C🍽me For
Everything

...but cholent!

By Kay Kantor Pomerantz

Come For Cholent
Come For Cholent Again

C🛎me For Everything

...but cholent!

*For Dr Ari
Joseph
Paley — בס"ד ב/רל?

My new/old KC חבר
fondly, Kay Kantor Pomerantz*

By Kay Kantor Pomerantz

Bloch Publishing Company
New York, New York

Published by Bloch Publishing Co., Inc.
37 West 26th Street, New York, NY 10010

Manufactured in the United States of America.

Library of Congress Cataloging-in-Publication Data

Pomerantz, Kay Kantor.
        Come for everything but cholent:/Kay Kantor
Pomerantz.
        p. cm.
        ISBN 0-8197-0615-9 (pbk. : alk. paper)
        1. Cookery, Jewish   I. Title
        TX724.P55   1995   95-24943
        641.5'676--dc20   CIP

FOR MOSHE AND OUR CHILDREN:

Raquel Naami and Bill
Alisa Batya and Stephen
Ari Judah
Josef Ami

and

FOR THE NEXT GENERATION:

Benjamin Jacob, Eliana Rina Zehava
and Yonatan Chaim
and many more....

We may live without poetry, music and art;
We may live without conscience, and live
     without heart;
We may live without friends, we may live
     without books;
But civilized man cannot live without cooks.

He may live without books -- what is knowledge
     but grieving?
He may live without hope -- what is hope but
     deceiving?
He may live without love -- what is passion but
     pining?
But where is the man that can live without
     dining?

                       by Lord Lytton

Reprinted from *Aunt Babette's Cookbook,*
Foreign and Domestic Receipts For The Household.
Bloch Publishing Co., 1889.

TABLE OF CONTENTS

Please Note: Throughout this book, all recipes that are marked Light 'N Easy are low in salt, fat, cholesterol and calories.

HELLO AGAIN!

With the publication of *Come For Cholent* and *Come For Cholent Again*, I believed I had exhausted my *cholent* recipes and ingenuity, though not my obsession... but my publisher was urging me to write another cookbook. My nephew, Dr. David Kantor, came to the rescue. I loved his suggestion for Book III in the "Come For..." series, a collection of favorite family recipes entitled, *Come For Everything... But Cholent*.

However, as I began work on this new collection, *cholent* recipes and stories continued to arrive. I confess that *cholent* is not "out of my system." Try as I did, I couldn't resist including a <u>final</u> *cholent* chapter!

I also pay tribute in this volume to the 100th-plus anniversary of the first cookbook printed by Bloch Publishing, *Aunt Babette's Cookbook*, by including some of "Aunt Babette's" menus, recipes and household hints throughout this book. (I have not personally tested "Aunt Babette's" recipes, but using a little imagination and taking a little chance, you may be delightfully surprised!) "Aunt Babette" called her cookbook "a valuable collection of receipts and hints for the housewife, many of which are not to be found elsewhere." The cooking oven on the front cover is taken from an advertisement appearing in her book.

As always, I hope you will find sustenance, enlightenment, fragrance and humor in these pages. (And, if you do, please tell your friends!) Enjoy!
                                                        KKP

ACKNOWLEDGEMENTS

Many people accompanied me in the writing of this book and their voices are often intertwined with mine.

-Family, all of whom shared recipes and traditions that have made up my own culinary heritage.

-Friends and colleagues, for their recipes, cheerleading and support; especially Robert Abramson for inspiration and counsel.

-Charles Bloch, whose friendship did not cloud his objective scrutiny.

-Amy Feigenbaum, for her cover design and artistic input.

-Tom Funk, artist, for his incredibly original work.

-Lois Goldrich, for her superb and careful reading.

-Shelley Kniaz, who improved this book markedly with suggestions, insights and brilliant editing.

-Dorothy Nathan, who once again brought my manuscript to life and whose critical faculties are evident throughout.

-Moshe, Ari and Joey, for the patience they displayed waiting for this book and for their humor and enthusiasm.

May you all be blessed with the same love and caring you have shown me. Thank you.

PREFACE

From *Aunt Babette's Cookbook*, Bloch Publishing

"In compiling these receipts, dear reader, it never occurred to me that the public would ever lay eyes on them. I hoarded them up as treasures for my own daughters and grandchildren. I think it the duty of every woman to be the head of her household, as much as it is the duty of the man to be the head of his place of business or counting room. It is indeed a woman's duty to see that nothing goes to waste, and food improperly prepared is a waste; and what is still more important the health of every member of the family depends on properly selected and prepared food, made palatable by seasoning, and that not too highly.

Many ladies may tell you that they did not know how to make a cup of tea when they got married, and pride themselves on being excellent 'cooks and housekeepers' now. Well and good, all honor is due them for their industry and perseverance, but they probably never told you of the heartaches and restless nights of worry it caused them...."

Aunt Babette, 1889

GLOSSARY

benchers	(booklets containing prayers after eating)
birkat hamazon	(prayer after eating)
blintzes	(crepes)
bubbie	(grandma)
cholent	(a Sabbath stew)
eingemahts	(preserves)
erev	(the preceding evening...)
fleisch	(meat)
freilah	(joyous)
griben	(Yiddish for fried chicken skins)
hahnasat orhim	(welcoming guests)
hallah	(egg bread)
haroset	(thick paste of ground nuts, apples & wine for Passover)
kartoffel	(potato)
kashering	(to make kosher)
keineinhora	(without the evil eye)
kichel	(curved, air-filled cookies)
kiddush	("sanctification," prayer recited over a cup of wine to consecrate the Sabbath or Festival)
kishke	(stuffed derma)
knaidle	(*matzah* ball)
kreplah	(wontons)
kugel	(usually noodles, rice, ground potatoes or vegetables baked in a casserole)
latkes	(potato pancakes)
l'hayim	(to life, "cheers")
lokshen	(noodles)

iv

maḥatenesteh	(a female in-law)
maḥatonim	(plural, in-laws)
maḥuten	(a male in-law)
meḥayeh	(such a pleasure)
milḥig	(dairy)
parve	(not meat, not milk)
Pesaḥ	(Passover)
riben	(grating)
Shabbat	(Sabbath)
Shavuot	(Weeks, Festival of the Giving of the Torah)
shul	(synagogue)
simḥah	(a joyous occasion)
sukkah	(a booth, hut)
Sukkot	(Festival of booths)
tzimmes	(a combination of ingredients cooked together, traditionally carrots)
yoiḥ	(Yiddish for soup)

CHAPTER I

SENSATIONAL
SOUPS

Rav said: A meal without salt is no meal.

Rabbi Ḥiyya bar Abba said: A meal without **SOUP** is no meal.

-Babylonian Talmud, tractate Berakhot, page 44a

- Make Mine Chicken Soup
- Summer Soup
- Strawberry *Borscht*
- Blueberry Soup
- Mama's Spinach Soup
- Carrot Soup
- Creamed Carrot Soup
- Wine Soup
- Asparagus-Leek Soup
- Avocado Soup
- Sweet and Sour Cabbage *Borscht*
- Chilled Cucumber Soup
- Lo-Cal Vegetable Soup
- Peanut Soup
- Buttermilk *Borscht*
- Chilled Fruit Soup
- Purim Soup
- Tomato Soup
- Vegetable Soup (Meat)
- Minestrone (Meat)
- Cream of Mushroom
- Almond Bisque
- Fish Chowder
- Herring Soup

BEER SOUP WITH MILK

Boil separately a quart each of beer and milk; sweeten the beer, add cinnamon, the crust of a rye loaf and the grated rind of a lemon; beat up the yolks of two eggs, add the milk gradually to the eggs, then the beer. Serve in small bowls.

Aunt Babette

MAKE MINE CHICKEN SOUP

As a young *rebbetzin* in Seattle, Washington, I was often asked for my recipe for chicken soup -- glorious golden *yoiḥ* -- the traditional *Shabbat* and holiday fare. It was simply expected that preparing this delicacy would be an area of my expertise. I learned from my mother, of blessed memory, that the delicately rich taste is due not only to the flavor of onions and carrots and other root vegetables, but to the whole chicken that goes into its making. Chicken soup is so popular that many a Yiddish writer and poet laud its aroma, flavor and glint in tales of grand wedding feasts or in praise of the holy *Shabbat*.

My prize recipe was first published in *Make Mine Chicken Soup*, the Herzl-Ner Tamid Sisterhood cookbook, in 1971. That was also the year I invented a game that has become not only a family favorite but one shared with countless guests over the years. The game requires making *knaidlaḥ* (*matzah* balls) for chicken soup and inserting a raisin in the center of several of the *knaidlaḥ* as they are being prepared. Once inserted, those *knaidlaḥ*, of course, look like all the others. When serving, someone (usually one of our children) eagerly announces that whoever finds a raisin in the center of his or her *knaidle* must tell a story, teach a song, share an anecdote or else help wash the dishes! Needless to say, guests have shared many wonderful stories, jokes and songs with us over the years.

Chicken soup:

1 chicken, cut up
12 cups water
3 carrots, cut in rounds
3 onions, quartered
1 celery root or 6 celery
  stalks and leaves
2 parsnips, cut in
  rounds (optional)
salt & white pepper, to
  taste

Place chicken in pot with water, season and put to boil and then skim. Add other ingredients and cook on a low heat until the chicken and vegetables are well done. If desired, strain the soup and add additional salt and pepper, to taste. Serves 10-12.

Knaidlah (*matzah* balls):

3 large eggs, separated
1 1/2 T. oil (or melted
  chicken fat)
1 t. salt
3/4 cup *matzah* meal

Beat egg whites until stiff. Beat yolks and fold into whites. Add the rest of the ingredients. Let stand in refrigerator for 10 minutes. Oil hands and form mixture into small balls. Drop them into rapidly boiling chicken soup. Bring to a rolling boil, cover and reduce to simmer for 20 minutes. Makes about 12. Recipe may be doubled. Note: My daughters have taught me a terrific time saver: commercially prepared kosher *knaidlah* mixes. I must confess -- not only are their *knaidlah* light and fluffy -- they're quite tasty.

SUMMER SOUP

During our sabbatical in Israel in '83, lovely neighbors invited us over for this refreshing, fat-free summer soup.

3 cups honeydew melon, cut-up
3 cups cantaloupe, cut-up
1/4 cup vodka or dry white wine
1/4 cup brown sugar
4 t. lime (or lemon) juice
3/4 cup strawberries, sliced

Place honeydew in blender and process until smooth. Pour into a bowl. Repeat with cantaloupe and pour into a separate bowl. Add 2 T. vodka, 2 T. sugar and 2 t. lime juice to each bowl. Stir and chill in refrigerator. To make 4 servings, pour 1/2 cup of honeydew mixture into each of 4 bowls. Next, pour 1/2 cup of cantaloupe mixture into center of honeydew mix. Garnish each bowl with a ring of sliced strawberries. Serves 4.

STRAWBERRY BORSCHT (Dairy)

Beautiful and delicious!

2 cups well-mashed or puréed strawberries
2 cups water
6 T. strained orange juice
2 well-beaten eggs
5 T. low-fat sour cream
sugar to taste, about 1 T.

Mix all ingredients until well blended. Chill until icy cold. Serves 4.

BLUEBERRY SOUP

Jane Epstein, early childhood educator, author and friend discovered this delicious and unusual soup from Norway. It's sure to appeal to the eye as well as to the palate.

3 1/2 cups fresh or 2 10-oz packages frozen unsweetened blueberries
1 cup granulated sugar
1/8 t. salt

medium piece lemon peel
2 T. potato flour (optional)
heavy or whipping cream (optional)

Early in the day, in a large kettle, combine blueberries with 1 1/2 quarts cold water, sugar, salt and lemon peel. Bring to a boil, then simmer, covered, about 15 minutes, or until berries are tender. Pour berry mixture through a strainer, mashing berries with a spoon; discard pulp left in strainer.

(Optional) Mix potato flour with 3 T. cold water. Bring blueberry mixture to a boil, stir in flour mixture, then cook, stirring, about 5 minutes, or until slightly thickened. Refrigerate, covered.

At serving time, remove lemon peel. Serve soup with a dollop of whipped cream (optional). Serves as a first course or as dessert with cookies. Makes 6-8 servings.

MAMA'S SPINACH SOUP

This delectable recipe is from my favorite express bus buddy, Jeanne P. Becker.

"I grew up eating this (and loving it), but being an Italian 'princess,' I was never allowed in the kitchen, and, therefore, when I got married, I had no idea how to make it. After 30 years of marriage, I finally figured out the recipe and now we enjoy it at least once every two weeks. (Italian princesses are kind of slow finding out how to operate on their own in the kitchen. Our mothers tell us, 'Time enough to do it when you have to.' They don't realize that when we have to, we don't know how.)"

4 cups (32 oz.) *parve* "chicken" broth
1 can or 1 package frozen chopped spinach
1 clove of garlic, diced or smashed

1 T. olive oil
2 large or 4 small potatoes, diced
grated parmesan cheese
Italian or French bread

Sauté garlic in olive oil. Add broth, spinach and potatoes. Cook on medium heat until potatoes are tender. Sprinkle with grated cheese and serve with warm bread.

CARROT SOUP (*Parve*)

For flavor, color and cost, carrots are most appealing!

1 lb. carrots, peeled
 and chopped
2 cloves garlic, minced
1 cup coconut milk
2 t. sugar

1 T. lime (or lemon)
 juice
salt & pepper, to taste
1/4 t. curry

In a saucepan, cover carrots with water and simmer until tender. Drain and blend with garlic, lime and one cup water until smooth. Return carrot pureé to saucepan and mix in remaining ingredients. Simmer 2 or 3 minutes. May be garnished with thinly sliced cucumbers or thinly sliced scallions. Serves 6.

CREAMED CARROT SOUP (Meat)

2 lbs. carrots, peeled
 and cut into chunks
2 potatoes, peeled and
 cut into chunks
6 cups chicken stock

3 cups liquid *parve*
 milk substitute
1 1/2 T. *parve*
 margarine
2 or 3 T. fresh parsley,
 chopped

Boil the carrots, onions and potatoes in the chicken soup for 5 minutes. Reduce heat to simmer for 30 minutes. Pureé mixture, add *parve* milk substitute and margarine and mix. Bring to a simmer and serve with parsley. Serves 8.

Come For Everything ... But *Cholent*

WINE SOUP

This soup is delicious hot or cold and may be garnished (for dairy meals) with a dollop of sour cream. Serves 4.

1 cup orange juice
1 1/2 cup cold water
3 T. honey
pinch of salt
1 T. cornstarch

1 cup wine (red or
  white grape juice
  may be substituted)
2 T. lemon juice

Bring to boil the orange juice, 1 1/2 cup water, honey and salt. Mix the cornstarch with the remaining 1/4 cup water and stir into the liquid. Continue simmering, stirring constantly until smooth, clear and creamy. Chill prior to serving.

ASPARAGUS-LEEK SOUP

Thanks to Ceil Skydell, a public relations consultant, this recipe has become a Pomerantz family favorite!

12 asparagus stems
  (remove tips)
2 leeks, chopped

1 onion, cubed
1 potato, cubed
4 T. margarine

Sauté asparagus tips in margarine and remove. Sauté remaining ingredients in margarine for 20 minutes. Add 3 1/2 cups of vegetable broth and cook until tender. Purée or process in food processor. Serve warm, garnished with asparagus tips.

MARAK AVOCADO -- AVOCADO SOUP

Make good use of extra chicken soup in the following delicious recipe. Cooking time is only about 4 minutes!

6 cups chicken soup
1 lb. soft avocado, diced
1 cup white wine (dry is best)

juice of 1/2 lemon
salt & pepper, to taste
1 sprig dill, optional

Put the soup, avocado and seasoning in the blender until smooth. Add the wine and lemon juice and heat (but do not boil), stirring well. Garnish with lemon slices. This soup serves 8. As always, enjoy!

SWEET & SOUR CABBAGE *BORSCHT* (Meat)

A filling, savory soup.

1 lb. flanken meat and marrow bones
2 1/2 lbs. cabbage, shredded
1 large onion sliced

1 large can tomatoes
juice of 1 lemon
brown sugar, to taste
salt & pepper, to taste

Boil meat and bones in 4 or 5 quarts of water for 1 hour and skim surface of soup. Add all ingredients except for lemon and sugar and simmer for 2 hours. Add brown sugar and lemon to taste and simmer for an additional 10 minutes. Serves 8.

CHILLED CUCUMBER SOUP (Dairy)

Great flavor and texture for cool summer refreshment (or anytime).

2 cucumbers, peeled, seeded and sliced
1 1/2 cup low-fat or non-fat yogurt

2 cloves garlic
2 T. dill, fresh or dry
salt & pepper, to taste
1/4 c. walnuts

Place cucumbers, garlic and yogurt in blender and blend until smooth. Add dill, salt and pepper and blend for 30 seconds. Chill. Garnish with walnuts before serving. Serves four.

LO-CAL VEGETABLE SOUP (*Parve*)

This soup is as bright as a *serape*.

1/2 cup chopped onions
1 cup celery plus leaves
4 cups water
salt & pepper, to taste
1/2 cup carrots, sliced

1/2 cup cabbage, shredded
2 cups tomato juice
1 t. *parve* chicken soup mix
dash of paprika

Simmer for one hour. Purée in blender until all vegetables are puréed. May be served hot or cold. Serves 6.

PEANUT SOUP (Dairy)

Different and delicious and oh-so-easy to prepare!

4 cups *parve* vegetable stock (instant or fresh)
1 onion, diced
1/3 cup peanut butter
2 T. margarine or butter
1/3 cup celery, diced

1 cup milk (skim, low-fat or whole)
1/3 cup flour
1/3 cup water
salt & pepper, to taste
chopped peanuts, unsalted

Cook vegetable stock, onion, celery, peanut butter, butter, and salt and pepper in a covered, heavy soup pot for several hours on low heat. In a bowl mix milk, flour and water and add to pot. Stir to mix well. Cook an additional 10 minutes and stir frequently. To serve, garnish with chopped peanuts. Serves 4.

BUTTERMILK BORSCHT

Drained canned beets
1 cup buttermilk
1/4 cup low- or non-fat cottage cheese

1 t. lemon juice
1/8 t. salt
ice cubes

For two servings, put 1/2 cup beets and remaining ingredients in blender with 1/2 cup ice cubes for 30 seconds. Serve in mugs or bowls. Garnish with thin cucumber slices.

CHILLED FRUIT SOUP (*Parve* or Dairy)

Try any combination of the following:

apples	apricots
quinces	figs
plums	grapes
strawberries	melons
raspberries	peaches
cherries	pears

3 cups of any of the
   fruits above, washed,
   pitted and chopped
8 cups water
3 T. cornstarch

sugar, to taste
3 cups orange juice
lemon juice, to taste
chilled dry wine
   (optional)

Bring fruits, water and sugar to a boil and simmer until tender. Press through a sieve and return to heat. Add the juices to taste. Dilute cornstarch in a small amount of water. Add to mixture and bring to a boil. Cool and refrigerate. (Add wine just before serving.) Serve cold and garnish with a sprig of fresh mint or, if dairy, a dollop of sour cream. Serves 8.

The following six soups are adapted, with permission, from *The Original Jewish Cookbook*, Mildred G. Bellin, Bloch Publishing Company.

PURIM SOUP -- FROM ISRAEL (Meat)

1 lb. beef brisket	5 small florets of
2 soup bones	cauliflower
1 quart water	1 t. sour salt
2 leeks (white part) in	2 egg yolks, well
strips	beaten in a soup
1 cup tomato juice	tureen
2 T. sugar	salt & pepper, to taste

Place meat, bones, and water in a soup kettle, bring to a boil, then simmer, covered, until the meat is very tender. Strain the broth and skim off the fat. Add remaining ingredients except egg yolks, bring to a boil once more, then cook over medium heat until the vegetables are tender, about 15 minutes. Taste, and make more sweet and sour by adding more sugar and sour salt or lemon, if desired. Slowly pour the soup over the egg yolks, stirring constantly. Serve at once. Serves 5.

TOMATO SOUP (Meat)

2 lbs. flanken	1 large onion
6 cups tomato juice	2 bay leaves
1 1/4 cups tomato	6 whole cloves
purée	2 T. sugar
2 cups water	salt & pepper, to taste

Place all ingredients in a large soup kettle, bring to a boil over high heat, then cook, covered, over low heat for 2 1/2 hours, until the meat is very tender. Strain. Serves 6. It may be served plain, or with cooked fine noodles or rice.

VEGETABLE SOUP (Meat)

1 1/2 quarts chicken
  soup
2 cups canned
  tomatoes
1/2 cup each (fresh or
  frozen) peas, cut
  green beans, whole
  kernel corn, baby
  lima beans

1/2 cup diced celery
1/2 cup diced onions
  or leeks
1/2 cup diced carrots
salt & pepper, to taste

Place all ingredients in a soup kettle, and cook, covered, about 20 minutes, until the vegetables are tender-crisp. For a heartier soup, add 1 cup of cooked rice or noodles. Serves 6 or more.

MINESTRONE (Meat)

A thick, hearty soup.

1 1/2 quarts beef stock
2 medium tomatoes,
  peeled and cut
1/2 cup shredded
  cabbage
1/2 cup diced onion or
  leeks
4 stalks celery with
  leaves, diced
1 can kidney beans

1 t. salt
1 clove garlic, minced
2 T. parsley, minced
1/4 cup carrots, diced
1/2 cup spinach,
  chopped
1/2 cup peas (fresh or
  frozen)
1 t. sweet basil, minced
pepper to taste

Place all ingredients in a soup kettle and cook about 20 minutes, until the vegetables are tender-crisp. For a *milhig* (dairy) soup, use water plus 2 tablespoons of olive oil in place of the beef stock, and serve with grated Parmesan cheese. Serves 6.

CREAM OF MUSHROOM SOUP (Dairy)

2 T. butter
1/2 lb. mushrooms,
  finely chopped
2 T. all-purpose flour
2 cups water
1 t. salt

1 egg yolk, slightly
  beaten
1/4 cup light cream
1 cup milk
1 t. onion salt

Melt the butter in a 2-quart saucepan. Add the mushrooms, cover, and cook on low heat for 10 minutes. Add the flour, blend thoroughly, and cook 1 minute, stirring constantly. Add the water and salt, bring to a boil, then lower the heat further and simmer 15 minutes. Blend the egg yolk with the cream. Add milk and stir. Heat to the boiling point and stir in the onion and salt. Serve garnished with minced parsley and paprika. Serves 4.

ALMOND BISQUE (Dairy)

1/2 lb. blanched
  almonds
3 cups hot milk
1 T. butter

1 T. all-purpose flour
3/4 t. salt
1 cup whipping cream
minced parsley

Grind or pound the almonds to a fine powder. Place in a saucepan with 1 cup of the milk and simmer for 5 minutes. In a separate saucepan, melt the butter, stir in the flour, and cook and stir over low heat until the mixture bubbles. Add the remaining milk and salt and cook and stir until thickened. Add the almond mixture and simmer 5 minutes while you whip the cream into stiff peaks. Remove from heat. Add the whipped cream and sprinkle a little minced parsley on each portion just before serving. Serve hot or cold. Serves 5.

FISH CHOWDER (Dairy)

A delicious, warming chowder.

1 very large potato,
  peeled
4 T. margarine or
  butter
1 medium onion, sliced

1 1/2 cups water
1 lb. fillet of cod, cubed
1 1/2 cups milk
salt & pepper, to taste

Cut the potato into 1/2" cubes. Melt the margarine in a 2-quart saucepan over medium-high heat. Add the potato, onion, and water, and cook, covered, about 20 minutes, until the vegetables are tender but still retain their shape. Add the fish and cook for 10 minutes longer. Add the milk, lower the heat, and simmer 5 minutes. Season to taste with salt and pepper. Serves 5.

HERRING SOUP, RUSSIAN STYLE (Dairy)

You will especially enjoy this soup when you are cold and very hungry.

2 herring, soaked and
  filleted (or 1 6-oz. jar)
2 cups milk

2 cups water
1 small onion, sliced
1/4 t. black pepper

Cut herring into tiny bite-sized pieces. Place all ingredients in a 2-quart saucepan, bring to a boil, then simmer, uncovered, for 15 minutes. Serves 6.

CHICKEN SOUP -- A SURE CURE!

One of the classic stories -- which has survived to this day -- is about the mother who bought two live chickens. When she came home, she discovered that one of the chickens was sick. She did what any woman with a mother's heart would do -- she made chicken soup from the healthy chicken and fed it to the sick chicken!

The less you eat in the evening, the sounder you will sleep.

Penine Hamelitzot

CHAPTER II

MAKE YOUR OWN LOX & OTHER FISH DELIGHTS

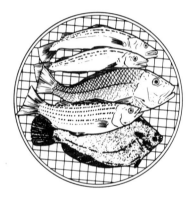

Eat a third and drink a third and leave the remaining third of your stomach empty.

Then, when you get angry, there will be sufficient room for your rage.

-Babylonian Talmud, tractate Gittin, page 70a

- Salmon, the King
- Seattle Salmon
- Home-Made Lox
- Lox Spread
- Pickled Salmon
- Marinated Salmon
- Sweet and Sour Salmon
- Poached Salmon
- Poached Fish
- Halibut Cheeks with Pasta
- Garlicky Baked Cod
- Fresh Tuna with Onions
- Babette's Tuna
- Tuna Salad
- *Gefilte* Fish
- Seared Snapper
- Herring with *Schnapps*
- Cod with Sautéed Almonds
- Citrus Fish
- Fresh Cod Burgers
- Orange Roughy With Oriental Sauce
- Ceviche

HAERINGSALAT

"Take six fine milch herrings, remove the heads and the skin, and take out the *milch*, which must be reserved for sauce; remove every bit of meat from the bones of the herrings, and soak it and the *milch* in milk over night (you may use water, but milk is better); chop up the herrings, not too fine, and chop equally as much nice cold roast veal, which ought to be tender and white; chop a few pickles and about four nice, large sour apples; boil about ten eggs hard, reserving four of these for decoration; add a few pieces of preserved or candied ginger, and a small cup of capers, also a few olives; chop everything separately, but not too fine, and put all these ingredients into a porcelain bowl and pour the following sauce over it: Rub the *milch* of the herrings to a cream, then rub it through a fine wire sieve; rub the yolks of two hard-boiled eggs to a cream, add a grated onion (a very small one), a spoonful of prepared mustard, a little white wine and vinegar, a pinch of salt, two tablespoonfuls of brown sugar and pour over the salad. Next day, before decorating, mix up well. For decorating, chop up the yolks and whites of eggs separately; line each dish with a lettuce leaf (for I think it the most practical to serve individual dishes of salads), put a layer of white, then a layer of yellow chopped eggs on each dish. To accomplish this easily, take a piece of pasteboard or the the blade of a knife in your left hand, and hold in line as you would a ruler, putting an olive in the center of each dish. This salad may be improved by adding all kinds of nuts chopped up."

Aunt Babette

SALMON, THE KING!

Living in Seattle for over 18 years intensified my affection for fresh fish, especially salmon. I learned that the many varieties of salmon -- including red, white, silver, coho, king, and so on -- could be poached, grilled, broiled, fried, blackened, marinated, pickled or cured into lox. Our first week in Seattle, we ate salmon 3 times a day. It was the first time we tasted fresh salmon, that is, not from a can, and we couldn't get enough of it. We snacked on Indian candy -- the tips of salmon, hard-cured and served up in long skinny strips at the Pike Place Market. In Seattle you even learn to make *gefilte* fish with salmon. May it forever swim upstream!

There are five species of Pacific Salmon.
  •KING: These are the largest and rarest of the five Pacific Ocean species. Their average weight is 18-20 pounds, although there are 40 pounders too. Their flesh is red or white. Seattleites claim white King is the best. The Kings from Alaska's Yukon and Columbia River are called CHINOOKS and are rich in flavor.
  •SOCKEYE or red: These weigh between 3-6 pounds and are a little less fatty than the King Salmon.
  •COHO or silver: These weigh from 2-12 pounds and are very tasty.
  •PINK, or humpback: These are the smallest salmon, averaging about 4 pounds, and are the most abundant of the five species. This type is generally canned.

•CHUM, or dog: These weigh 8-10 pounds and are best known for their eggs, which are sold as salmon caviar. (*Ikura*, a layer of salmon caviar atop rice, is my favorite sushi, only surpassed by salmon skin rolls -- sheer ambrosia!)

SEATTLE SALMON

Yes, I know there are a million ways to prepare salmon, even in Seattle -- but this is the easiest, tastiest and most delicious. The best part is that it looks like you've spent all day fussing over it. A great company pleaser.

> Place 1 salmon fillet (1 1/2" thick) on a foil covered cookie sheet, skin-side down. Smear with a light paste of mayonnaise, lemon juice and seasoned salt. Place under broiler for 7 minutes or until brown. Turn off oven and allow fish to rest in closed oven for an additional 15 minutes. Plan on 3 to 6 ounces per individual serving.

HOME-MADE LOX

Our family adopted "Aunt" Augusta of blessed memory. A number of personal tragedies left her completely alone. She was never lonely because she sought to do acts of loving-kindness for everyone she knew. The baby clothes she crocheted for my children are now being worn by my grandchildren. The programs she embraced are being carried on in her name.

Augusta loved salty foods and made delicious pickles, but best of all was her home-made lox. She taught me how to take fresh salmon, rub it down with a special paste and cure it. We made over 80 lbs. of it when my son, Ari, became a *Bar Mitzvah*, and even more than that when Joey became a *Bar Mitzvah*.

Most of the year I have home-made lox in the freezer for under $5 per pound.

First, select a nice fillet of salmon. King salmon (red) is the best for making lox. The fillet should be thick -- at least 1 1/2 - 2", although thinner fillets work. This recipe is based on a mixture of ingredients for each 2 1/2 lbs. of fish.

Method:
Rinse salmon and pat dry with paper towels. Place skin side down on heavy duty foil. Prepare a "paste" of the following ingredients:

8 t. coarse salt	1 t. liquid smoke
2 T. brown sugar	1/2 t. oil

Note: If mixture seems too dry, add a few more drops of liquid smoke and oil.

Seal foil tightly and place in refrigerator, skin side down at first, and allow it to "cure" for 2 weeks. After the first week, unwrap and turn salmon over. Rub any remaining juices over salmon and seal tightly for a second week.

When cured, salmon should be partially frozen for ease in slicing. Slice at an angle and refreeze immediately. Wrap packets in freezer wrap, saran wrap or foil, in individual or family-size servings. Enjoy.

LOX SPREAD

A little goes a long way.

1/2 lb. lox (odds 'n ends are great!)	1 cup real or imitation sour cream
1/2 cup minced onion	2 t. white horseradish
3 t. chopped dill	dash lemon juice

Mix all ingredients and adjust to taste. Cover and allow to refrigerate at least one hour.

PICKLED SALMON

This mouth-watering recipe is delicious and an easy make-ahead treat for company or family.

4 lb. salmon, cut in chunks	1 jar sweet pickles (medium) cut in chunks
1 bottle ketchup (medium)	1 onion, sliced
1/3 cup brown sugar	2 t. pickling spice (tied in bag)
juice of 2 lemons	

Bring sauce to a boil, add fish and cook 15 minutes. Cool and refrigerate for 2 days before serving. Serve cold. An excellent selection for a buffet table.

MARINATED SALMON

A tasty treat to be served as an appetizer on top of shredded lettuce.

2 lbs. fresh salmon	pepper
1/4 cup sugar	dill
1/4 cup kosher salt	

Mix salt, pepper and sugar in deep bowl. Put layer of dill and some of the salt, pepper and sugar mixture into the bowl. Slice fish into bite-sized pieces and place in bowl, skin down. Sprinkle on more seasoning mixture. Put a board or plate and stone on top and refrigerate overnight.

SWEET AND SOUR SALMON

Variations for the sweet and sour sauce in this recipe guarantee my family will never tire of this popular entreé. Try adding 2 tablespoons vinegar to the water in which fish is simmered, along with a teaspoon of mixed pickling spices; or substitute a half cup of wine for half of the fish broth in preparation of the sauce. Simply scrumptious!

2 lbs. salmon (or white fish)	6 gingersnap cookies (optional)
1 1/2 t. salt	4 T. vinegar
boiling water	4 T. brown sugar
2 cups fresh fish broth or instant imitation chicken soup	4 T. raisins
	2 T. almonds, sliced
	1 T. vegetable oil
	lemon juice

Sprinkle salmon with salt and cover with boiling water. Cook gently in a large shallow pan for 20 minutes. Remove from water.

To prepare sweet and sour sauce, measure out 1 1/2 cups of the fish broth and all ingredients except the lemon juice and cook in a saucepan for 10 minutes or until smooth. Season to taste with salt and pepper and lemon juice and, if desired, additional sugar. Pour the sauce over fish and serve hot or cold. Serves 5.

POACHED SALMON

Remember that outlandish idea of poaching a salmon by wrapping the fish tightly and placing it on the upper rack of the dishwasher for an entire cycle? (Without soap, of course!) You're right, I had to try it with a small piece of fish and can report that it does work. However, in all honesty, we were nervous about sampling it.

However, here's an alternative -- a tasty, yet simple way to poach a salmon that's guaranteed to please.

For a 3-4 lb. piece of fresh salmon, you'll need a tall can of tomato or V-8 juice (no other seasonings) and a fish poacher (or suitable large stove-top pan). Empty the juice into the pan and bring to a boil. Place the fish on a rack in the juice. When it boils again, reduce heat and allow to simmer for 15 minutes. Remove from heat and allow fish to cool. Drain and remove skin as desired. Place on a serving dish and garnish with fresh lemon and parsley. Allow a minimum of four ounces per person.

POACHED FISH

A delicate, light dish permeated with the experience of centuries.

4 lbs. sea bass, salmon
   or trout, cut in fillets
1 large carrot, chopped
1 celery stalk, chopped
1 medium onion,
   chopped

1 garlic clove, chopped
1 cup white wine
1 T. white wine
   vinegar
olive oil
salt & pepper, to taste

Pour 6 cups of water into a large non-stick skillet. Add all ingredients except for fish and bring to a boil. Simmer for 15 minutes. Place fish in skillet, skin side down, and poach on simmer for approximately 10 minutes. Remove the fish with a large slotted spatula and place on serving platter. Brush with olive oil. (If desired, skin may be removed prior to brushing with oil.) Serve with a tangy cocktail sauce, combining equal parts of ketchup and horseradish or with *Salsa Verde*, page 136.

HALIBUT CHEEKS WITH PASTA
AND SUN-DRIED TOMATOES

This dish is light but totally infused with flavor. I get hungry just thinking about preparing it!

1 lb. halibut cheeks cut into thin strips
1 cup low-salt *parve* vegetable broth
1 1/2 oz. sun-dried tomatoes (about 15)
2 T. dry white wine
1 t. basil

1 t. olive oil
1/4 t. salt
1/4 t. pepper
4 cups hot cooked spaghetti (8 oz.)
1 1/2 oz. (6 T.) reduced fat white cheese, grated

Combine vegetable broth and tomatoes in a one-cup glass measuring cup. Cover with plastic wrap for the microwave with a vent. Microwave at high for 3 minutes. Allow to rest 5 minutes. Remove tomatoes and chop. Place halibut, wine, basil, oil and salt and pepper into a 2-quart casserole and stir well. Cover with plastic wrap for microwave with vent and cook in microwave for 4-5 minutes until halibut is tender. Add tomatoes, spaghetti and cheese and toss well. Serves 4.

GARLICKY BAKED COD

Today when there are garlic festivals and even garlic ice cream, one need not worry about garlic breath. Having garlic on your breath is now a badge of good taste -- so enjoy!

1 1/2 lbs. cod, cut into chunks
1/2 cup bread crumbs
3 T. parsley, chopped
1 t. lemon rind, grated
3 cloves garlic, minced

2 T. lemon juice
4 t. olive oil
salt & pepper, to taste
vegetable cooking spray

Coat 4 individual baking cups with cooking spray. Divide fish equally in cups and set aside. Combine the bread crumbs, parsley, lemon rind, salt and pepper and garlic in a bowl, stir in lemon juice and oil. Sprinkle this mixture evenly over the fish. Place baking cups on a baking sheet and bake at 375° for 12-15 minutes. Bread crumbs should be lightly browned. Serves 4.

FRESH TUNA WITH TANGY ONIONS

You'll forget about the canned variety once you've experienced this fresh tuna.

8 4-oz. tuna steaks (about 3/4" thick)
2 cups onions, chopped
1 T. olive oil
1/2 cup red wine vinegar
1/2 cup all-purpose flour
2 t. olive oil
salt & pepper, to taste
mint or parsley for garnish

Heat one tablespoon oil in a large non-stick skillet over medium heat. Add onion and sauté for 4-5 minutes. Add vinegar, salt and pepper and cook for approximately 2 minutes or until most of the liquid evaporates. Remove and set aside. Wipe skillet with paper and continue. Combine flour and a dash of salt and pepper in a shallow dish. Dredge tuna in flour. Heat 2 teaspoons oil in skillet over medium heat. Add tuna and cook for 2 minutes on each side for medium-rare. (Cook longer if desired.) Serve with onion mixture and garnish with mint or parsley. Serves 8.

BABETTE'S TUNA

Our children's very own "Aunt Babette" is my wonderful Seattle friend, Babette Schiller.

2 lbs. fresh tuna
1/4 cup sherry
1/4 cup lime juice
2 t. garlic, minced

1 T. oil
1 1/4 t. chili powder
1/2 t. dry mustard
1/2 t. grated lime rind

Marinate tuna at least 4 hours. Bake at 350° for 10 minutes. (Can also be barbecued.) Do not overcook. "Tuna is best when served rare." Babette.

GOOD FOR YOU TUNA SALAD

A healthful version of an old favorite.

1 can (12 oz.) solid white tuna in water, drained
1/2 cup plain, low-fat yogurt
1/2 cup carrots, finely shredded

1/2 cup celery, finely chopped
1 t. lemon zest (colored part of peel), grated
freshly ground pepper, to taste

In a bowl, break up tuna with fork. Add remaining ingredients and mix well. Refrigerate until ready to serve. Serves 4.

LITTLE NANA'S *GEFILTE* FISH

Nana (also known as Sara Eckstein) became a part of our lives when our daughter, Cantor Alisa Pomerantz, married Stephen Boro. Next to my mother's recipe -- also prepared by Ann Kaye of Bellevue, WA -- this is the best *gefilte* fish ever!

On day prior to cooking fish, wash and lightly salt fish and bones. Place paper towels between layers of fish. Cover loosely and place in refrigerator.

In a big pot prepare and set aside:

1 parsley root	salt & white pepper to
1 onion	taste
2 celery stalks	enough water to cover
3 cubes of sugar	bottom of pot

For the fish:

1 lb. whitefish	3 sugar cubes,
1 lb. pike	dissolved in hot
1 lb. winter carp	water
1 onion, sliced	1/2 glass ice water
1/4 cup *matzah* meal	4 large carrots
2 eggs	Fish bones

This recipe may be doubled as many times as you'd like.

Fillet fish and cut into strips. Dry and lightly salt the fish. In food processor or grinder, grind fish a little at a time, alternating with slices of onion to push fish through and to add flavor. Save some onion for the end to push all the fish out. Add

---

matzah meal, eggs and dissolved sugar cubes to ground fish. Mix and chop the fish mixture for at least one-half hour. Add one drop of the ice water at a time as you chop to enhance the consistency of the mixture. (You will use a total of approximately 1/4 cup of the ice water.) Add salt and pepper to taste. When the fish sticks to the chopper, it is a sign that it is ready. Bring pot of water and veggies to a boil. Pat fish into ovals the size of your palm and place in a layer on the boiling water. When the first layer turns white, add the next layer on top. Add fish bones after an hour and cover with layer of carrots. Cook for an additional hour. When cool, remove fish to a serving tray and garnish with slices of carrot, cut on the diagonal. Strain some fish soup over tray and reserve remainder in a container. Recipe makes 15-20 pieces.

"Little Nana's *Gefilte* Fish has been a staple of every holiday meal since I was a little girl. Every batch is better than the one before -- and on Passover, it is especially tasty. Nana credits the pots she uses, but I think it's the elbow grease that goes into the chopping. It wouldn't be a family get-together without Nana's *Gefilte* Fish."

Lisa Boro Greenberg

SEARED SNAPPER WITH MANGO AND BLACK BEAN SALSA

This lip-smacking gourmet dish is from our son Joey, who is now in the C.I.A. -- the Culinary Institute of America.

6 6-oz. snapper fillets (with skin removed)

<u>Mango and Black Bean Salsa:</u>
In advance: Combine all ingredients for salsa, mix well and refrigerate until needed.

1 cup cooked black beans, drained	2 tomatoes, diced
1 large mango, diced	1/2 cup lemon juice
1 cup red onion, diced	1/2 cup orange juice
1/2 bunch cilantro, chopped	1/3 cup lime juice
	salt & freshly ground pepper, to taste

<u>Honeydew Marinade:</u> (Purée)

2 T. olive oil	1 onion, diced
6 cloves garlic, chopped	1/2 bunch cilantro
	2 shallots
1 1/2 T. red wine vinegar	2 cups honeydew melon
1 yellow bell pepper, diced	1/2 cup water
	2 T. lemon juice
1 red bell pepper, diced	salt & freshly ground pepper, to taste

Heat a large non-stick sauté pan over medium high heat. Add olive oil and sear peppers, onions, shallots and garlic. Place in food processor and purée, scraping down the sides of the bowl as needed. Add remainding ingredients and process

→

to combine. Adjust the seasoning with salt and pepper.

Snapper:
To prepare the fish, heat a non-stick sauté pan over medium-high heat. Brush the snapper fillets with soy sauce, then dip the fillets into the honeydew marinade. Sear briefly, until nearly cooked through. Serve topped with mango and black bean salsa. Garnish each serving with a sprig of cilantro. Serves six.

HERRING WITH SCHNAPPS
by Francis Blumenfeld (adapted from a recipe by Faygie Morse, Toledo, Ohio)

Great for the festival of *Shavuot* or for a break-the-fast supper.

1 large jar herring in wine sauce (16 oz.) or a 1 lb. fresh pickled herring	16 oz. sour cream 1 1/2 oz. rye whiskey 1 1/2 oz. Scotch 1 cup sugar
3 yellow onions, thinly sliced	1 lemon, sliced in quarters

Remove herring from jar and discard sauce and onions. Wash herring under cold water. Mix liquor with sour cream. Add herring and onions. Stir well in bowl and refrigerate for 8 hours. Stir occasionally during the 8 hours. Add lemon and place in a glass jar for storage. This herring delicacy will keep for weeks in the refrigerator.

FILLET OF COD WITH SAUTÉED ALMONDS

This favorite entree helps get dinner on the table fast. It is a simple, healthy main course that can be prepared in 15 minutes or less. Add a salad and quick rice and enjoy.

1 1/2 lbs. cod fillet
1 cup flour
1/4 t. salt
1/8 t. pepper
1 T. vegetable oil

1 T. butter
1/2 cup slivered
  almonds
1 1/2 T. lime juice
1 lime (sliced)

Place the flour on a plate or board and mix in salt and pepper. Dredge both sides of each fish fillet in flour and shake off excess flour. Heat the oil (over medium heat) in a large non-stick skillet. Sauté the fillets until golden brown on each side (approximately 3 minutes per side) and remove to a warm serving plate. (A bit more oil or oil spray may be added, if needed.) Add the butter to the skillet to sauté the almonds over moderate heat for about 3 minutes, stirring constantly. Pour the lime juice over the nuts and simmer for one minute. Sprinkle the almonds on top of the cod and serve with the lime slices. Serves 4.

CITRUS FISH

You'll love the radiating citrus flavor in this dish.

4 fresh tuna, salmon or firm-fleshed fish steaks	1 T. lemon peel, grated
	1 T. orange peel, grated
1 stick margarine	1 t. mint, chopped

Allow margarine to soften to room temperature. With fork, blend in lemon and orange peel and chopped mint. Form margarine into log, cover with plastic wrap and refrigerate. When firm, cut into 1/2" slices. Broil or grill fish fillets on one side for 4 minutes. Turn over. Place 1 or 2 slices of margarine on each slice of fish and broil or grill for an additional 4 minutes. Serves 4.

FRESH COD BURGERS

My own version of Baltimore's famous "coddies." My husband, Moshe, says these <u>must</u> be eaten between crackers, as a sandwich. I suggest buns.

1 1/2 lbs. cod, ground	1 T. lemon juice
1/2 onion, ground	1 T. mustard
1/3 cup *matzah* meal or bread crumbs	1 egg
	salt & pepper, to taste

Mix all ingredients thoroughly. Wet hands and shape into 4 patties and chill 20 minutes. Grill outdoors or sauté in large skillet which has been coated with vegetable oil spray. Spread sandwich buns with mustard, add lettuce and "coddies." Serves 4.

ORANGE ROUGHY WITH ORIENTAL SAUCE

Another tangy fresh fish recipe from Babette Schiller.

2 lbs. orange roughy	1 T. lemon juice
1/4 cup orange juice	1 clove garlic, minced
2 T. oil	1/8 t. pepper, white
2 T. light soy sauce	

Marinate fish one hour. Place fish on lightly oiled grill or barbecue, or broil in oven. Brush fish frequently while cooking. Serves 4-5.

CEVICHE

Another raw fish dish I learned to make while living in Mexico City many years ago. Today, I prepare this delicacy while listening to *Macarena*. Delicious served as a first-course appetizer on a bed of lettuce. In Mexico it was often served with yucca roots, which I understand are also available in California and some parts of the Midwest.

First, in a bowl, place 2 lbs. sea bass, halibut or firm whitefish. Cut in 1" cubes, no skin, no bones. Cover with lemon juice and season with salt and pepper.

Next, slice 2 onions and rinse in salt water and drain. Place in a second bowl and cover with lemon. Add a finely diced tomato. Pour onions over fish and allow to marinate in refrigerator overnight.

CHAPTER III

CHICKEN AND MEAT SPECIALTIES

Ben Sira gives advice on how to control oneself at a dinner party overflowing with tempting food.

> If you are sitting at a grand table, do not lick your lips and exclaim, "What a spread!..."

> Do not reach for everything you see or jostle your fellow-guest at the dish; judge his feelings by your own and always behave considerately....

> If you are dining in a large company, do not reach out your hand before others.

> A person of good upbringing is content with little, and is not short of breath when he goes to bed.

> The moderate eater enjoys healthy sleep and rises early, feeling refreshed.

> But sleeplessness, indigestion, and colic are the lot of the glutton.

-Wisdom of Ben Sira, ch. 31, verses 12-15 and 18-20.

- Chicken With Figs
- Pineapple Chicken
- Chicken Salad Surprise
- Fall-Apart Chicken
- Sweet and Sour Chicken
- Orange Chicken Stew
- Shirley's Chicken
- Apricot Ginger Chicken
- Mini-Chicken Drumsticks
- Temma's Lemon Chicken
- Beef-Artichoke Marinade
- Chinese-Style Ribs
- BBQ Lamb Riblets
- Curried Beef or Lamb
- Hamburger Yummy
- Wieners in Whiskey
- Turkey Dumplings
- Turkey Breast With Cranberries
- Brisket and Beer
- Sweetbread Croquettes
- Teriyaki Steak
- Sweet and Sour Meat Balls

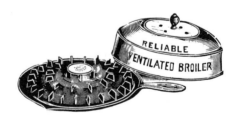

JUST FOR FUN!

The following 6 recipes have been reprinted from *Aunt Babette's Cookbook.*

FLEISCH KUGEL (MEAT BALL)

Two pounds of beef, chopped extremely fine (the round is best); have half a pound of suet chopped with it, and get your butcher to chop two onions in with the meat, it will be mixed better. Season with salt, pepper and half a loaf of grated stale bread, half soaked in water and then pressed well and dried in hot fat before adding to the meat; break in two eggs and mix thoroughly, mould into a huge ball, put into a deep iron *kugel* form or spider, which has been well greased and heated before putting in the *kugel*; dip a spoon in cold water to smooth the top of the *kugel*, put flakes of fat on the top and bake about two hours, basting often.

BRISKET OF BEEF

No. 1. Take about five pounds of fat, young beef (you may make soup stock of it first), then take out the bones, salt it well and lay in the bottom of a porcelain-lined kettle and put a quart of nice sauerkraut on top of it and let it boil slowly until tender; add more vinegar if necessary, thicken with a grated raw potato and add a little brown sugar; some like a few carroway seeds added.

BRISKET OF BEEF

No. 2. May be prepared in numerous ways. After taking it out of the soup, you may prepare it with a horseradish sauce, garlic sauce, onion sauce, etc.

HASHED CALF'S LUNG AND HEART

Lay the lung and heart in water for half an hour; then put on to boil in a soup kettle with your soup meat intended for dinner. When soft, remove from the soup and chop up quite fine. Heat a spoonful of goose fat in a spider; chop up an onion very fine and add to the heated fat; when yellow, add the hashed lung and heart; salt and pepper; add soup stock and thicken with flour. You may prepare this sweet and sour by adding a little vinegar and brown sugar and a tablespoonful of molasses; boil slowly; keep covered until ready to serve. Very nice.

SPICED VEAL LOAF

Chop up three pounds of veal very fine (let your butcher chop it for you); roll six crackers very fine; beat up three eggs light, and season highly with salt, pepper, ginger and nutmeg; mix all this thoroughly, not forgetting to add a tablespoonful of goose fat; press all into a baking pan, about four inches high; grease the pan well and put lumps of goose fat on top. Bake about three hours, basting frequently. When cold, this is very nice; cut into thin slices.

STEWED VEAL

Wash a breast of veal; wipe it dry and sprinkle with a mixture of fine salt and ginger. Heat some goose fat in a stew pan; cut up an onion in it; add sliced parsley root or celery; when hot, lay in the breast of veal, cover up air tight and stew a few minutes; remove the lid and turn the veal on the other side; now add one or two tomatoes cut up, or a table-spoonful of canned tomatoes and a very little hot water; cover up tight again and stew slowly and steadily for two hours, turning the meat often. When done, thicken the gravy with a teaspoonful of flour, wet in a little cold water; add minced parsley or carroway seed; boil up once and serve. Mashed potatoes and green peas or stewed tomatoes are usually served with veal.

VEAL SWEETBREADS (FRIED)

Wash and lay your sweetbreads in slightly salted cold water for half an hour; pull off carefully all the outer skin; wipe dry; sprinkle with salt and pepper. Heat some goose fat in a spider, lay in the sweet-breads and fry slowly on the back of the stove, turning frequently until they are a nice brown. You may roll them in cracker crumbs and then in beaten egg, seasoned with salt.

CHICKEN WITH FIGS

I am a devout matchmaker! This delicious recipe comes from Debbie Astor and Bill Dantzic (a recent success story!)

2 chickens (2 1/2 - 3 lbs. each) cut into 8 pieces each (or equivalent breasts and thighs)
6 large cloves garlic, finely minced
2 T. dried thyme
1 T. ground cumin
1 t. ground dried or grated fresh ginger
1 t. salt
1/2 cup red wine vinegar
1/2 cup best quality olive oil
1 1/2 cups dried apricots*
1 cup small figs or large fig pieces
1/2 cup packed brown sugar
1/2 cup Madeira or Cabernet Sauvignon
1 cup large pecan pieces
grated zest of 2 lemons

Combine chicken, thyme, cumin, ginger, salt, vinegar, oil, apricots and figs in a large bowl. Cover and marinate in the refrigerator overnight. Remove from refrigerator one hour before cooking. Preheat the oven to 350°. Arrange the chicken in a single layer in a large shallow baking pan. Spoon the marinade mixture evenly over the chicken. Sprinkle with the brown sugar and pour the wine between the pieces. Cover the pan tightly with aluminum foil and bake for 40 minutes. Remove foil and continue baking for an additional 20 to 30 minutes, basting to keep moist, until chicken begins to brown and juices run clear when a thigh is pierced. When done, transfer chicken and fruit to a large platter. Drizzle with a few large spoonfuls of pan juices, sprinkle with pecan pieces and then with lemon zest. Pass remaining pan juices in a gravy boat. Serves 6.

*"If you don't have dried apricots (we didn't), we found about 3 tablespoons of duck sauce a very satisfactory substitute for taste and flavor."

PINEAPPLE CHICKEN

An easy baked chicken dish that is outrageously delicious.

2 1/2 lbs. chicken, cut up
1/4 t. celery salt
1/4 t. nutmeg
1/4 t. garlic powder

1 1/2 T. *parve* margarine
2 cans (or 1 lb.) sliced pineapple in syrup
2 T. soy sauce

Wash and dry chicken. Mix seasonings and rub into chicken. Melt margarine in a large baking pan. Arrange chicken skin-side down in a single layer. Bake uncovered at 425° for 30 minutes. Turn chicken skin-side up. Drain pineapple syrup and add to soy sauce. Pour over chicken and bake for 15 minutes. Add pineapple slices and bake 10 more minutes. Serves 4.

CHICKEN SALAD SURPRISE

This delicious salad is from our son Ari, who is a production assistant at M.T.V.

Salad:

1/2 lb. cooked chicken, cubed
1/2 sweet onion, diced
1 T. sautéed garlic, diced
2 scallions, diced

1 8-oz. can hearts of palm, drained and chopped
1 8-oz. can artichoke hearts, drained and chopped

Dressing:

1 small can anchovies, drained and diced (anchovy paste may be substituted)

1/4 cup lemon juice
1/8 cup olive oil
salt & pepper, to taste

Thoroughly mix all ingredients for dressing and refrigerate. Assemble all ingredients for salad and toss with dressing. Adjust salt and pepper to taste. Serves 2-3.

FALL-APART CHICKEN

This savory chicken recipe is by Ann Kaye. Ann, whose maiden name is Pomerantz, called in search of relatives from her home town of Bereza Kartuzka. As Jewish geography would have it, after some discussion, we learned Ann was related not to my husband but to my mother's family -- the Ditkowiczes of Bereza. Go figure!

2 chickens, cut in 8ths
8 large garlic cloves,
   sliced
1 large onion, sliced

2 peeled oranges,
   sliced
1 large apple, sliced

Put the sliced garlic, oranges, onion and apple into a roasting pan. Add salt and pepper to taste. Cover pan and put aside. Prepare chicken by cutting away excess fat (removing the skin is optional). Place cut chicken on broiler pan and broil slightly. Add chicken to the ingredients in the roasting pan, mix, and cover. Bake at 350° for about 2 hours. Remove chicken from the roasting pan and set aside. Put gravy through a sieve and pour over chicken. Serves 6.

NOTE: For those concerned with fat intake, chill gravy in refrigerator until fat forms on the surface. Then skim off fat, heat, and pour over chicken.

SWEET AND SOUR CHICKEN

Our friends, Elaine and Dr. Harold Kellner, love experimenting with this recipe. To date, Elaine has substituted beef, veal and tofu in place of the chicken. Harold has enjoyed tasting each new variety and urges her to continue her creativity.

1 1/2 lbs. chicken (cut up pieces or cutlet chunks)
1 cup vinegar
1 cup water
3/4 t. salt and a dash of pepper

3 green peppers
2 cups canned pineapple chunks
1 cup sugar
2 tomatoes
3 T. corn starch
3 T. ketchup
2 T. oil

Batter
2 eggs
3/4 cup flour

1/2 t. salt
2 T. water

Cut green peppers diagonally into about 8 pieces each. Cut tomatoes in wedges, 8 pieces each. Set aside.

Make a batter by mixing eggs, flour, salt and water. Mix well and dip chicken into batter. Remove and fry in hot oil until golden brown. When chicken is ready, set aside.

Place all ingredients except tomato and chicken in pot and mix well. Bring to a boil, add chicken and tomato, mix thoroughly and cook 3 minutes. Serves 4.

ORANGE CHICKEN STEW

This stew can be made several days in advance and kept refrigerated. It's also delicious reheated and served with a glass of cold beer. It's definitely worth the fuss!

2 lbs. chicken cutlets
2 cups orange sauce*
4 T. unsalted *parve*
  margarine
3 medium red peppers,
  chopped
1 medium red onion,
  sliced
2 T. flour
4 cups chicken stock

2 lbs. sweet potatoes,
  peeled and cut into
  chunks
1 1/2 T. salt
1 lb. tomatoes,
  chopped
1 cup fresh or frozen
  corn kernels
1 cup parsley, chopped
1 t. orange zest

Place the chicken and one cup of orange sauce in a glass bowl. Turn the chicken and coat well. Marinate in refrigerator for 2 hours or overnight. Grill or broil the chicken for 3-4 minutes per side, cover and cut into 1" chunks. In a large casserole, melt the margarine over medium heat. Add the peppers and onion and cook about 6 minutes. Sprinkle the flour over the vegetables and stir for 2 minutes. Stir in the chicken stock, sweet potatoes and salt and the remaining cup of orange sauce. Bring to a boil and then reduce to simmer for 30 minutes. Stir in the tomatoes, corn, parsley and orange zest. Return the chicken to the pot and cook for 5 minutes. Season to taste. Serves 6-8.

*Orange Sauce recipe follows on next page.

Orange Sauce:
(This recipe makes 3-4 cups and can be stored in the refrigerator as a marinade for meat or poultry.)

4 T. *parve* margarine	2 t. salt
1 large onion, chopped	1 1/2 t. black pepper
6 garlic cloves, minced	1 t. cumin
1 cup honey	2 cups chicken stock
1/2 cup tomato paste	1 cup orange juice
2 T. lemon juice	

Mix all ingredients. Bring to a boil and simmer for 3-4 minutes. Cover and set aside.

SHIRLEY'S CHICKEN

Very seldom will a synagogue caterer share a treasured recipe. This one was a favorite from Pacific Northwest Sisterhood luncheons.

1/3 cup frozen orange juice concentrate	1 egg, slightly beaten
1 t. salt	3 lb. chicken, cut up

Mix first 3 ingredients, add chicken and marinate 15 minutes.

Mix:

1 cup crushed corn flakes	1/2 cup shredded coconut
1 t. curry powder	

Remove chicken from marinade and coat with above mixture. Place chicken on lightly oiled pan and drizzle with leftover marinade. Cover and bake at 350° for 30 minutes. Remove cover and bake an additional 30 minutes.

APRICOT GINGER CHICKEN

This family favorite is assertively seasoned and is super-satisfying!

2 chickens, cut up
1/3 cup flour
1/4 cup oil
1 T. ginger
1 T. garlic powder
1/3 cup sherry

salt & pepper, to taste
1 large can apricot
   halves in
   unsweetened juice
1/2 lemon, sliced thin

Coat chicken parts with flour. Heat oil in a large frying pan and brown chicken on all sides, about 15 minutes. Sprinkle ginger, garlic, salt and pepper over chicken and place in a baking pan, skin-side up. Pour sherry and undrained apricots in frying pan, mix with pan juices and pour over chicken. Place lemon slices on chicken and bake in a pre-heated 350° oven for 45 minutes or until chicken is tender. Serves 8 or more.

MINI-CHICKEN DRUMSTICK APPETIZERS

A friend helped me make these a few Sundays ago. The aroma brought in neighbors I hadn't seen in months!

To make 24 mini-appetizers:

12 chicken wings	2 T. sherry
1/2 cup soy sauce	2 cloves garlic, minced
1/2 cup water	1 t. fresh ginger
2 T. sugar	

First, cut off the wing tips and reserve or freeze for making chicken soup at a later time. The remainder of the wing is cut in half at the joint and the meat and skin are pushed up on the bone of each section. (In the small half of wing there are two bones. Remove smaller bone after cutting loose and discard.) Place drumsticks in a flat baking dish. Combine all ingredients and pour over wings. Marinate 1 or 2 hours or overnight.

Preheat oven to 350° and bake chicken in marinade for 45-50 minutes or until done. Turn drumsticks midway through the baking.

TEMMA KINGSLEY'S LEMON CHICKEN

"When I was growing up, my father always made the turkey gravy. I knew that he used sage and thyme for seasoning. Later, the first *Erev Shabbat* after our honeymoon I asked my husband, Al, to pick up a cut-up chicken (the only kind I knew how to cook). When he brought home a whole chicken I didn't know what to do with it. Fortunately, the Settlement cook book, my one and only cookbook at the time, had a basic roast chicken recipe which I followed with the addition of sage and thyme. Since my mother always put an orange inside a turkey, I decided to try a lemon -- and it's been a tradition in our home for 30 years!

1 large chicken (whole)	garlic, salt, sage,
2 lemons	thyme, poultry
1 cup water	seasoning, to taste

Cut lemons in half and place in cavity of chicken. Sprinkle liberally with garlic, salt, sage, thyme and poultry seasoning. Place on rack in roasting pan. Put water in bottom of pan. Roast at 400° for 1 1/2 hours. Baste once or twice. Squeeze lemons into gravy boat and fill with pan drippings from which fat has been skimmed. Serve on the side. Great with mashed potatoes."

BEEF-ARTICHOKE MARINADE

This is a company-favorite creation by Aunt Bete, my husband Moshe's sister, who is a terrific cook. (Isn't it fun that even as adults we call family members by their relationship to our children, rather than to us?)

1 1/2 - 2 lbs. beef, veal or lamb cubes
1 large onion, sliced
2 red peppers, sliced
2 6-oz. jars of marinated artichoke hearts

3 T. ketchup (low salt)
1/2 cup beef or chicken bouillon
1/4 t. cumin
1/2 t. garlic, chopped
1/2 package powdered artificial sweetener

Cut onion into small wedges. Cut red peppers into 1" slices. Drain marinade from both jars of artichoke hearts and place in large pot. Brown meat in the marinade until nearly tender and remove from pot. Brown onion and red peppers in the same pot, stirring frequently until tender-crisp, and remove. Add all other ingredients to pot and stir thoroughly. Return meat and vegetables to pot, cover and simmer on low flame until meat is fork-tender. If more liquid is needed, add more bouillon. Serves 6-8.

RIBS ON THE RUN!

Our sons have taught me you can never serve too many ribs! Here are a few of their favorites.

CHINESE-STYLE RIBS

4 lbs. beef ribs
1/3 cup soy sauce
2 T. ketchup

1/3 cup orange marmalade
2 cloves garlic, crushed

Place ribs on a foil-lined baking tray. In a bowl, mix all ingredients. Brush sauce on both sides of meat. Bake in 350° oven for one hour. Stop to baste every 15-20 minutes. Cover with foil to retain moisture.

BBQ LAMB RIBLETS

4 lbs. lamb ribs
1 large onion, sliced
2 cloves garlic, minced

1 cup barbecue sauce
salt & pepper, to taste

Place ribs in broiler pan in oven to brown and remove excess fat. Sprinkle ribs with salt and pepper and place on a foil-lined baking tray. Add onion, garlic and barbecue sauce. Bake in 350° oven for one hour. Stop to baste every 15-20 minutes. Cover with foil to keep moist.

CURRIED BEEF OR LAMB

Great flavor -- great taste!

2 lbs. beef or lamb,
   cubed
2 T. oil

1 cup tomatoes or
   tomato sauce

Spices:
2 T. curry powder
1/4 t. dry mustard
1 medium onion,
   chopped
1/4 cup parsley

1 or 2 cloves garlic,
   chopped
1 T. sugar
salt & pepper, to taste

In a heavy dutch oven, fry spices in oil until onions are tender. Add meat and stir for 15 minutes. Add tomatoes, cover and simmer for one hour. If desired, thicken with a *roux* (a thin paste) of flour and some of the liquid in the pan and cook an additional 30 minutes. Serve with boiled rice, a sprinkling of raisins and coconut.

JUDY'S HAMBURGER YUMMY

Judy Amiel's Sephardic roots no doubt inspired this delicious dish.

1 onion, chopped	2 T. parsley
3 stalks celery,	3 T. *matzah* meal
chopped	6 beaten eggs
2 lbs. hamburger	1 can tomato sauce

Sauté onion and celery. Add hamburger and mash. Cook until meat browns. Add eggs, parsley and tomato sauce. Grease 9"x13" pan with oil. Place in 400° oven until oil heats. Sprinkle with *matzah* meal. Add meat mixture. Bake 40 minutes. Serves 8 or more.

WIENERS IN WHISKEY

You won't believe this taste sensation!

1 lb. hot dogs	1 cup ketchup
3/4 cup brown sugar	3/4 cup whiskey

Simmer hot dogs in whiskey for 20 minutes. Cocktail-size hot dogs cooked this way make a terrific appetizer.

TURKEY DUMPLINGS

Invented by our daughter Cantor Alisa and her husband Stephen in San Diego and shared with us.

1 egg, beaten
1 lb. ground turkey
2 T. soy sauce
2 T. cooking sherry
2 T. sesame oil
1 t. white pepper
2 t. minced garlic
1 t. ginger (fresh)
1 pinch of sugar
1 t. salt

1 T. cornstarch
1 small can water chestnuts, chopped
2 scallions, chopped
2 packages wonton wrappers
wok
bamboo steamer basket(s)
oil spray

Mix all ingredients. Place small dollop of mixture in center of wrapper. Dip your finger in water and rub on edge of wrapper and fold over to seal. Then turn ends up and set aside. Place 2 inches of water in a wok and bring to a boil. In a bamboo steamer basket that has been lightly sprayed with cooking oil, place single layer of dumplings. When water is at full boil, place steamer basket in wok. Reduce heat and simmer for 15 minutes. Remove and serve immediately with dumpling sauce (citrus-seasoned soy sauce).

If you have more filling remaining, pat into bite-size "meatballs" or flattened "hamburgers" and grill or broil -- absolutely delicious!

TURKEY BREAST WITH CRANBERRIES

Delicious and colorful for Thanksgiving or any time of the year.

1 frozen turkey breast,
  partially thawed
2 T. cornstarch
1/2 cup orange
  marmalade

1/4 cup sugar
1 cup fresh cranberries,
  processed or
  chopped
salt & pepper, to taste

In a saucepan, mix cornstarch and sugar, then add cranberries and marmalade. Stir until mixture thickens and bubbles. Put turkey breast in roaster and sprinkle with salt and pepper. Pour the hot sauce over turkey and cover. Bake at 325°, according to weight of turkey. Slice and serve with sauce.

BRISKET AND BEER

Any beer will do nicely. I have also tried this with Israeli dark beer (tastes like root beer) and enjoyed its fragrance and flavor. *L'ḥayim!*

3-5 lbs. brisket, lean	1/2 cup chili sauce
1 onion, sliced	1 bottle beer
2/3 cup celery, chopped	salt & pepper, to taste

Put meat in a heavy dutch oven or roaster. Mix all ingredients except beer. Pour mixture over meat. Pour the beer over all. Cover and slow-cook on stove top for 3-4 hours or in 350° oven for 2 1/2 hours, until tender.

This may also be cooked in a crockpot (slow-cooker) on high for 4-5 hours or on low for 8-10 hours. When ready, allow meat to cool, then slice and serve with its juice. Serves 8-10.

SWEETBREAD CROQUETTES

I grew up noshing on sweetbreads and other "spare parts" that today are considered delicacies.

1 lb. sweetbreads	water
1 egg and 1/4 cup	salt & pepper, to taste
matzah meal for each	extra *matzah* meal and
cup of meat	1 beaten egg for light
1 T. vinegar	breading

Wash and soak sweetbreads for one hour in cold water to which 1 T. vinegar has been added. Remove from water and wash again. Boil sweetbreads in salted water for 20 minutes. Plunge into cold water. Drain and remove membranes and tubes. Chop fine. Add one slightly beaten egg, 1/4 cup of *matzah* meal and salt and pepper to each cup of meat. Form into patties, dip in beaten egg and roll in a little *matzah* meal. Broil or fry for several minutes on each side. (Also a delicious treat for *Pesaḥ*!)

TERIYAKI STEAK

This recipe is always a winner.

2 1/2 lbs. chuck steak

Marinate for 24 hours in a sauce made by combining:

1/2 cup soy sauce	1 T. Worcestershire
1/4 cup brown sugar	sauce
1/2 cup olive oil	1 cup water
1/4 cup sherry	1 clove garlic, minced

This makes a rich, flavorful sauce. A steak cut 1" thick will take 30-45 minutes to grill on the barbecue or under the broiler. Cook to desired doneness.

SWEET AND SOUR MEAT BALLS

Elaine Bieber sells books for the United Synagogue all week long, but her culinary skills shine on weekends. You're certain to enjoy these mouth-watering meat balls.

2 lbs. lean chopped veal (or beef)	1/2 cup rice, uncooked
2 eggs (optional)	5 cloves fresh garlic
1 bottle chili sauce, with equal amount of water	8 oz. grape jam and 4 oz. water
	1 _hallah_ roll, crumbed

Mix meat, eggs, garlic, bread crumbs and rice. In a large sauce pan, mix chili sauce and water, grape jam and water. Bring to a boil and simmer 20 minutes. Add meat balls to sauce and cook for 1 hour and 25 minutes. Serves 10.

CHAPTER IV

VEGETARIAN FAVORITES

ADVICE ON EXERCISE

Often, one does not consider exercise, though it is the main principle in keeping one's health and in the repulsion of most illnesses....

There is no such thing as excessive body movements and exercise, because body movements and exercise will ignite natural heat and superfluities will be formed in the body, but they will be expelled. However, when the body is at rest, the natural heat is suppressed and the superfluities remain....

Exercise removes the harm caused by most bad habits, which most people have. And no movement is as beneficial, according to the physicians, as body movements and exercise.

Exercise refers both to strong and weak movements, provided it is a movement that is vigorous and affects breathing, increasing it. Violent exercise causes fatigue, and not everyone can stand fatigue nor needs it. For the preservation of health, shorten the exercises.

-Maimonides, The Preservation of Youth

- Vegetarian Chili
- Mango Salad
- Tofu "Egg"less Salad
- Chinese Tofu Salad
- Frozen Cheese Salad
- Baked Cheese Blintz Loaf
- Fiesta Salad
- Overnight Omelette
- Broccoli Casserole
- Spinach Soufflé
- Broccoli Fettucini
- Vegetable Pie
- Zucchini Chow Mein
- Carrot Ring
- Artichoke Squares
- Cheese Spoon Dumplings
- Rice Casserole
- Cold Sesame Noodles
- Tomato With Baked Egg
- Mock Chopped "Liver"
- Eggplant Caviar
- Marakkesh Carrots
- Kale With Browned Garlic
- Smashed Rutabagas
- Orange Parsnips
- Baked Mushrooms
- Spicy Carrots

HINTS FROM AUNT BABETTE.

•HAVING ACCEPTED AN INVITATION TO DINNER, it is proper to be at the house half an hour previous to the time set for dining. And do not leave, under any circumstances, until half an hour after dining; however, a dinner party rarely breaks up until late, as music, games, etc., usually follow.

•CARE OF THE HANDS -- When your hands become badly stained from kitchen work, wash them first in cold water, then rub them well with dry powdered borax; now wash them with very warm water and lemon juice, cleaning the nails at the same time by rubbing them in the lemon. Before drying pour a few drops of glycerine into the palm of the hand and rub well into the skin and wipe perfectly dry. Do this before retiring at night and you will find that your hands will soon become soft and white.

•RAISINS should be cleaned dry by rubbing between two cloths.

•IT is a good plan to make parsley butter in the summer for winter's use. Melt the butter, boil until clarified, then throw in as much chopped parsley as you desire. It is very convenient to use in winter, when greens are scarce, for gravies, etc. You may do the same with goose or any other kind of fat.

•HOW TO PRESERVE "DILL" FOR YOUR WINTER PICK-LES -- Put fresh green dill in wide-mouthed jars and pour vinegar over it. You may use both the dill and vinegar on your pickles.

•AN uncomfortably tight shoe may be made perfectly easy by laying a cloth wet in hot water across where it pinches, changing several times. The leather will shape itself to the foot.

•WHEN putting away the silver tea or coffee-pot which is not in use every day, lay a stick across the top under the cover. This will permit fresh air to get in and prevent the mustiness that is so often found in them.

•TO CLEAN GLASS DECANTERS -- Crush egg shells into bits, put into the decanter three parts filled with cold water. Shake thoroughly up and down.

•A RIPE tomato will clean the hands after paring fruit. If very much stained use a lemon; digging your fingers into it will also clean your finger nails.

•SLICED ONIONS in a sick-room absorb all the germs and prevent contagion. It is a good plan to hang an onion in the nursery.

•EGG STAINS may be removed by rubbing with common table salt.

•TO REMOVE iron taste from new iron kettles, boil a handful of hay in them.

•OLD wall paper may be cleaned by rubbing with a loaf of stale bread. Cut the loaf in half and rub gently on the wall.

•IN putting away knives, wrap them in paper to prevent rusting. Never in woolen cloth.

•IN winter clean windows with a sponge dipped in alcohol.

•KEEP salt and pepper on a shelf near your cookstove; it will save you many a step.

•IN dusting a silk dress, never use a brush; wipe carefully with a piece of soft flannel, shaking the flannel occasionally.

•IN sewing, change your position frequently, it will help to rest the body.

•EAT salt with nuts, to aid digestion.

•YELLOW soap and whiting, mixed together in a little water into a thick paste, will effectually stop a leak in your boiler.

Thanks, Aunt Babette!

VEGETARIAN CHILI

The following three variations of this delectable treat are from Anaruth Bernard, my Detroit-Schechter Day School connection.

LONG METHOD:

1 cup dried red kidney beans

1/2 cup dried whole green lentils

1 T. oil

1 onion, peeled and chopped

1-2 garlic cloves, crushed

1 t. mild paprika

1 14-oz. can ground tomatoes

1/2 cup soy grits (TVP)

1-2 T. red chili powder

1 red pepper, roasted, seeded and chopped

salt & fresh ground pepper

The night before:
Place kidney beans in a bowl, cover with a generous amount of water and refrigerate overnight.

Next day:
Drain the beans and place in a pot with water to cover. Simmer 1 1/2 to 2 hours. (A strip of kombu makes the beans more digestible.) Simmer the dried lentils in a generous amount of water for 45 minutes. Drain the beans and the lentils and save the water. Sauté the onions and the garlic in oil. Add the tomatoes. In a pot, combine the tomato mixture with the beans, lentils and soy grits. Add paprika and chili powder. Simmer 15 minutes, adding reserved liquid as needed. During the last five minutes, add the roasted pepper. Season with salt and pepper. This freezes well.

→

FAST METHOD:
Substitute 2 15-oz. cans of red kidney beans. Can also purchase frozen chopped onions and "jar" garlic.

LOW FAT METHOD:
Substitute wine for oil to sauté the onions and garlic.

(I usually make a double or triple recipe using a red, an orange and a yellow pepper.)

MANGO SALAD

When time permits, the way to enjoy a whole ripe, peeled mango is to insert a mango fork into the fruit, get into the bathtub with it and slurp away! When you're in a hurry, this delicious mango salad is a terrific accompaniment to grilled meats and fish. I like it with scrambled eggs.

2 ripe mangoes, peeled and diced
1 large orange, peeled and sectioned
1 cup pineapple cubes

2 scallions, diced
1 T. apple cider vinegar
salt & pepper, to taste

Gently mix all ingredients. Cover and let sit at room temperature, allowing flavors to meld -- at least 30 minutes. Makes a minimum of 6 side-servings.

TOFU "EGG"LESS SALAD

Robin Freedman, mother of four children under the age of 10 who are in *shul* every week, devised this delicious mock egg salad. "It makes a great <u>h</u>allah sandwich!"

1 package firm tofu (10-16 oz.)	1/8 t. salt
3 t. mayonnaise (fat-free or regular)	dash of ground mustard
1/4 cup celery, minced	dash of paprika
1/8 t. curry powder	pepper, to taste
1/8 t. cumin	1 t. onion, minced (optional)
1/8 t. coriander	

Mash tofu with fork to consistency of your favorite egg salad. Mix in mayonnaise. Add spices, mixing well. Adjust seasoning to taste. Mix in celery (and onion, if desired).

CHINESE TOFU SALAD

A light salad that is very pleasant.

For salad:
4 cups thinly sliced red cabbage
1 or 2 packages tofu, cut in 1" chunks
1 cup carrots, julienned
1 cup scallions, julienned
1 T. toasted sesame seeds

For dressing:
1/4 cup plain low-fat or non-fat yogurt
1 T. tahini (sesame-seed paste)
2 t. soy sauce
1/2 t. ginger, ground or grated
1/2 t. garlic, ground or minced
salt & pepper, to taste

Make dressing by mixing all ingredients. In a large bowl, combine salad ingredients. Add dressing and toss to coat. Sprinkle with sesame seeds. Serves 4.

FROZEN CHEESE SALAD

A tempting June treat to herald the arrival of summer.

2 cups dry cottage cheese	10 stuffed olives, chopped
1/2 cup chopped walnuts	1/2 cup cream salt & pepper, to taste

Season cottage cheese with salt and pepper, to taste. Add walnuts and olives. Whip the cream and fold into cheese. Pack into a mold or oblong baking pan. When frozen, unmold and slice. Place slices on lettuce leaves and, for color, sprinkle with a small amount of paprika. Serves 4.

BAKED CHEESE BLINTZ LOAF

This delicious blintz loaf with half the fuss relieves a craving for blintzes.

Batter: Mix together

1/2 cup butter	1 1/4 cup flour
1/2 cup sugar	1 t. baking powder
2 eggs	1/2 t. salt
3/4 cup milk	

Filling: Mix together

1 lb. dry cottage cheese	1 t. sugar
2 T. butter	salt
1 egg	

Pour half of batter into oiled 9" baking pan. Layer with filling mixture. Pour remaining batter over filling and bake at 350° for 1 hour. Serves 8.

FIESTA SALAD
(Black beans and rice)

This change-of-pace salad will add an ¡*Olé*! to your day.

2 cups rice, cooked & chilled

1 can black beans, rinsed & drained

2 cups chopped peppers -- use red & yellow

1 cup celery, diced

1/2 cup onion, diced

1/2 t. cumin

1/2 cup cilantro, chopped

1/2 cup low-fat Italian dressing

1/4 cup hot sauce (or to taste)

juice of one lime (or lemon)

salt & pepper, to taste

Mix all ingredients thoroughly and chill overnight. Serves 6.

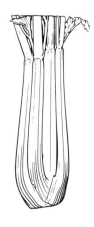

OVERNIGHT OMELETTE

I learned to make this fabulous dish for brunch from my sister-in-law, Shirley Ann Epsten of Kansas City. Incidently, she taught me a lot of other interesting things, too....

1 loaf _hallah_ (remove crust)
1/2 lb. Longhorn cheese
1/2 lb. Monterey Jack cheese
8 oz. cream cheese (can use fat-free)

10 eggs or egg beaters
2 cups milk (can use skim)
1 stick low-cal margarine
1/2 t. mustard (dry)
1 T. chives
salt & pepper, to taste

Spray 9"x13" rectangular pan with vegetable oil. Tear _hallah_ into small pieces and place in pan. Melt margarine and pour over _hallah_. Beat eggs and milk together. Mix in other ingredients and pour over cheese. Cut cream cheese into small pieces and place over top of mixture. Cover with foil and place in refrigerator overnight. Bake (covered with foil) at 325° for one hour. Remove cover and bake an additional 10-15 minutes (longer, if necessary) until brown. Serves 10-12.

BROCCOLI CASSEROLE

This recipe almost belongs in the "5 minutes or less" category. It's quick to put together, low in calories and quite filling.

1 cup cooked rice
1 cup cheddar cheese (reduced-fat), shredded
1/2 cup mushrooms, sliced
1/2 cup onion, diced
1/4 cup skim milk
4 t. margarine (reduced-calorie)
1/4 t. salt
dash pepper
2 packages (10 oz.) frozen chopped broccoli
vegetable oil spray

Combine everything except the broccoli in a saucepan and simmer until cheese melts (approximately 4-5 minutes). Stir frequently. Add the broccoli and cook an additional 2-3 minutes. Spray a 2-quart casserole, spoon in mixture and bake at 350° for 20-30 minutes. Serves 5.

SPINACH SOUFFLE (Dairy)

A delicious main course or accompaniment. A Sephardic variation includes the addition of one boiled (mashed) potato.

1 package frozen spinach (10 oz.)	1/2 t. salt
	1/2 t. pepper
1/4 cup margarine (or butter)	1 cup cheddar cheese (grated)
1/4 cup flour	1 T. onion, chopped
3/4 cup milk	4 eggs

Cook spinach. Make white sauce with margarine or butter, flour, milk, salt and pepper. Add to cheddar cheese. Then add cooked spinach and chopped onion. Separate eggs and add yolks to mixture. Let cool. Beat egg whites until they come to a peak. Fold into batter and place in a greased casserole. Bake for 30-35 minutes at 350°. Serves 6. This recipe may be doubled.

BROCCOLI FETTUCINE (Dairy)

Yogurt provides a rich sauce for this delicious creamy recipe, a real family favorite.

4-5 cups broccoli
  (small florets)
olive oil spray
2 cloves garlic
2 cups crushed
  tomatoes
1-2 t. anchovy paste
1/2 cup chopped
  onions

1/2 cup non-fat yogurt
2 t. cornstarch
1/2 cup ricotta cheese
1 lb. fettucine noodles
2 oz. grated parmesan
  cheese
ground pepper, to
  taste

Steam broccoli for 5 minutes until almost tender. Boil water for pasta. Heat large non-stick pan and spray with olive oil. Sauté garlic and onions for a second or two, add tomatoes, reduce heat and simmer. Add anchovy paste and broccoli, cover and turn off heat. Stir yogurt into the cornstarch a little at a time to keep smooth. Mix or blend with ricotta (in food processor, if desired). Cook fettucine and drain. Add yogurt mixture to pan with drained fettucine. Season with pepper and top with grated parmesan cheese. Serves 4.

VEGETABLE PIE (*Parve*)

Ceil Skydell says this recipe is as easy as one, two, three....

2 eggs or 3 egg whites
1 slice _hallah_ (softened in water)
soy sauce

1 16-oz. package of mixed vegetables (frozen)

Mix together. Bake in your favorite pie crust at 350° for 35-45 minutes. Serves 4.

ZUCCHINI CHOW MEIN

We've always had success growing zucchini in our summer garden. This recipe is yet another way to enjoy its abundance each summer.

1/4 cup margarine
1 cup sliced celery
1 large onion, sliced in thin rings

3 T. soy sauce
3-4 cups zucchini, cut in 1/4" rounds
2 cups bean sprouts

Melt margarine in skillet. Add celery, onions and zucchini. Cover and steam-fry over low heat until vegetables are fork-tender. Don't stir too often. Add soy sauce and bean sprouts. Cook until sprouts are heated through. Serve over hot rice or noodles. Serves 6.

CARROT RING

This recipe from Jane Epstein originated in Pittsfield, Massachusetts, in the early '60s. It's a delicious side dish enjoyed by her family and friends.

3/4 cup butter or margarine
1/2 cup brown sugar
1 egg
1 1/4 cup flour
1/2 t. salt

1 t. baking powder
1 t. baking soda
1 t. lemon juice
1 T. water
1 cup grated carrots (2-3 large ones)

Cream the butter and sugar. Add egg. Sift together and blend in flour, salt, baking powder and baking soda. Add lemon juice, water and carrots. Put into well-greased 6-cup mold and bake at 350° for 45 minutes. Serves 6.

Note: When mixing, first add liquids to part of the flour and other dry ingredients, then put in grated carrots for moisture, and add the remainder of the flour.

ARTICHOKE SQUARES

This delicious dish can be enjoyed all year long.

2 jars (6-oz.) marinated
  artichoke hearts
1 small onion, finely
  chopped
4 eggs, beaten with
  fork
1/4 cup fine dry bread
  crumbs

1 clove garlic, minced
1/4 t. salt
1/8 t. pepper, oregano,
  tabasco sauce
2 cups shredded
  cheddar cheese
2 T. chopped parsley

Drain liquid of 1 jar artichoke hearts into frying
pan. Chop artichokes and set aside. To the liquid
in the frying pan add onion and garlic. Sauté 5
minutes. Combine eggs, bread crumbs, salt, pepper, oregano, and tabasco sauce. Stir in the cheese,
parsley, onion mixture and remaining artichokes
and liquid. Grease a 9"x12" pan. Bake at 325° for 30
minutes. Cut into squares. Serve hot or cold.

CHEESE SPOON DUMPLINGS WITH RED PEPPER SAUCE

This cheese dish makes a great impression! It's what I call gourmet *Shavuot*. It's quite delicious all year 'round.

Sauce:

2 red peppers, cut in chunks
1 8-oz. can whole tomatoes
1 1/2 cups water (include juice from tomatoes)

1/2 t. salt
1/2 t. pepper
2 T. cornstarch, dissolved in 2 T. water
2 T. butter
2 T. olive oil

Cheese Dumplings:

4 quarts water
12 oz. ricotta cheese
1 t. salt
1 t. pepper
2 eggs

1/3 cup parmesan cheese
3/4 cup flour
2 T. chives, chopped

Sauce:
Bring the red peppers, tomatoes and water to a boil. Reduce to low, cover and steam for 12 minutes. Put mixture through a food mill. Return mixture to saucepan, stir in salt and pepper and cornstarch. Bring to a boil. Add the butter and oil and emulsify with a hand beater for 18 seconds. Set aside.

Dumplings:
Bring water to a boil in a large pot. Place all of the ingredients except for chives into the food processor. Process for 12 seconds. Transfer mixture to a

bowl and mix in the chives. Drop the batter, one tablespoon at a time, as quickly as possible, into the boiling water. When all the batter has been spooned into the water, reduce heat to low and simmer for approximately 10 minutes. (The dumplings will rise to the top of the water as they cook.) Remove dumplings to a platter with a slotted spoon.

For an appetizer, place 3 dumplings on a small plate and spoon on red pepper sauce. A slice or 2 of fresh red pepper is a pretty accompaniment. Serves 6.

RICE CASSEROLE

This recipe by Elaine Kellner can be pulled together in minutes and is simply delicious.

1 cup regular rice
  (uncooked)
1 can clear chicken
  soup*
1 can water
2 medium onions,
  diced (large pieces)

1 medium can
  mushrooms with
  liquid
1/4 cup *parve*
  margarine, melted

Brown onions in margarine. Mix all ingredients and bake in a covered 2-quart casserole at 350° for 1 hour 15 minutes. Stir every half-hour. Serves 4.

*To make recipe *parve*, use imitation chicken broth.

COLD SESAME NOODLES

Several members of our family were willing tasters and contributors to this recipe. Depending on who's cooking, this recipe varies from sweet to sweeter, tangy to tangier. It always tastes delicious!

4-5 T. peanut butter
1 T. sesame or tahini
  paste
3-4 T. brown sugar
1 t. ginger
1 T. vinegar
1-2 t. sherry wine
2-3 t. soy sauce

1 1/2 T. sesame seed
  oil
1-2 t. minced garlic
1/4-1/2 cup boiling
  water
1 lb. cooked spaghetti
  noodles

Mix all ingredients except noodles in a bowl. Pour sauce over noodles and lightly toss. Optional: garnish with grated carrots and chopped scallions.

TOMATO WITH BAKED EGG

Delicious for a lovely Fall brunch or as an appetizer, anytime at all.

For each serving you will need:

1 whole large tomato	seasoned bread
1 T. onion, finely	crumbs or *matzah*
chopped	meal
1 egg	salt & pepper, to taste

Select a large, firm tomato, cut off the top and scoop out the pulp. Salt inside, drain and sprinkle with onion. Fill half full with bread crumbs. Bake at 350° for 20 minutes and remove from oven. Crack an egg (checking for possible blood spots) into the tomato. Sprinkle with salt and pepper and return to oven until the egg is nicely set (approximately 10 minutes).

Come For Everything ... But *Cholent*

LOTSA MOCK CHOPPED LIVER (*Parve*)

These spreads can be used as an appetizer, dip or sandwich spread. (Some have been consumed for a complete lunch.) Which variation tastes most like chopped liver?

ISRAELI STYLE

1 large eggplant
5 hard-boiled eggs,
  chopped or grated
1 T. onion, grated

salt & pepper, to taste
a little oil in which
  some diced onion has
  been fried

Remove stem, split eggplant lengthwise and place cut-side down on a foil-lined cookie sheet. Place beneath broiler until fork-tender. Remove and allow to cool. Scoop out the insides (remove seeds, if desired) and mash well. Combine with all other ingredients. Taste and correct seasoning. May be served room temperature or chilled.

AMERICAN STYLE

2 cups cooked green
  beans, mashed
2 hard-boiled eggs,
  chopped or grated
1/3 cup walnuts,
  ground

1 T. *parve* margarine
1 T. wine
salt & pepper, to taste
a little oil in which
  some diced onion has
  been fried

Combine all ingredients and chill for best flavor.

MIRIAM BORO'S *MA͟HATENESTEH** STYLE

1 can peas, drained
3 small onions
2 hard-boiled eggs

16 walnuts
1/4 cup oil

Chop onion and sauté in oil until white and soft. Chop or blend rest of the ingredients, including oil from sautéed onions. Add salt and pepper to taste. If you want more, just double ingredients.

Place in refrigerator for at least 24 hours before serving so flavors can meld. Serve cold.

*When your children marry, you become in-laws (in Yiddish) *ma͟hatonim*, plural; *ma͟huten*, male, singular; *ma͟hatenesteh*, female, singular.

EGGPLANT CAVIAR

This Romanian recipe was inspired by my Aunt Sylvia.

1 medium eggplant
2 onions, minced
3 cloves garlic, crushed
salt & pepper, to taste

1 tomato, chopped
1/4 cup vegetable oil
vinegar, to taste
black olives

Wash, then bake or broil the whole eggplant until tender. (It will take about 20 minutes. Turn to cook evenly.) Remove from oven and peel the skin. Add all ingredients (except olives) to mixing bowl and chop fine. Season to taste. Serve on salad greens with olives as garnish. Serve as an appetizer, salad or cold vegetable. Serves 4 or 5.

MARAKKESH CARROTS

This recipe was inspired by many visits to Marakkesh in La Jolla, California. I'm not sure how they make it, but this recipe comes close in flavor and texture.

1 lb. carrots, peeled
  and sliced
1 1/2 T. lemon juice
1 t. ground cumin
1/4 t. ground
  coriander

1 1/2 t. sugar
salt & pepper, to taste
1 T. olive oil
1 T. chopped fresh
  coriander

In a saucepan, cover carrots with water and simmer 15 minutes until carrots are *al dente* (tender but slightly firm). Drain and place in a pretty bowl. Add the lemon juice and remaining ingredients and toss thoroughly. Cover and marinate several hours before serving. (Grated raw carrots may be substituted for the cooked carrots.) Serves 4 to 6 as a side dish.

KALE WITH BROWNED GARLIC

According to the United States Department of Agriculture, kale is a superfood. "It contains 300 milligrams of potassium, important in maintaining fluid balance and heart function." But that's not all. "One cup of kale also delivers more than 90 milligrams of calcium, 50 milligrams of vitamin C and the beta-carotene equivalent of more than 9,600 units of vitamin A. This high concentration of anti-oxidants makes it one of the most nutritious of all vegetables." It's so valuable, it's also listed now in the dictionary as slang for money!

1 bunch kale	water
4 large cloves garlic, chopped	1 1/2 t. olive oil

Wash kale thoroughly -- soak and rinse several times. Cook kale in boiling water until tender, drain and set aside. To brown garlic, heat oil in a non-stick skillet. Add chopped garlic and sauté 3 minutes or until browned. Be careful -- garlic burns quickly. Toss with kale. (Browned garlic is also delicious on asparagus, potatoes, artichokes and broccoli.) Serves 4.

SMASHED RUTABAGAS

This recipe is now a Thanksgiving tradition in our daughter Raquel and her husband Rabbi Bill Gershon's home, having been passed down from his family.

4 large rutabagas
1 1/2 cups water
1 t. sugar
margarine, as needed

parve non-dairy
creamer, as desired
salt & pepper, to taste

Peel and cut (carefully) rutabagas into chunks. Add water and sugar and cook covered until tender (about 20-30 minutes). Drain and mash with *parve* margarine, *parve* non-dairy creamer, and salt and pepper to taste to desired consistency.

Rutabaga (a yellow turnip), rich in vitamin C, also contributes calcium and several vitamins to the diet. It is inexpensive and plentiful all winter long. It is sold small (2 1/2 - 3 inches) to extra-large (5 inches or more). Select those with firm, yellow flesh and a deep purple "mantle." It takes 2 1/2 - 3 lbs. to serve 4-6 people. Young, tender rutabagas may be served raw.

ORANGE PARSNIPS OR CARROTS

Parsnips are an acquired taste. If they're a new taste treat for you, try this sauce first on carrots.

6 large parsnips or
   carrots, peeled and
   cut in thin sticks
water, to cover

salt & pepper, to taste
2 T. margarine
1/3 cup orange juice
1 1/2 T. honey

Cook parsnip sticks in seasoned water until tender. Drain and remove to serving platter. In a saucepan, melt the margarine and add the orange juice and honey. Bring to a boil. Pour sauce over parsnips before serving.

MUSHROOMS BAKED IN FOIL

Any type of mushroom will do. Serve as a tasty side dish.

1 lb. fresh mushrooms
1/4 cup chopped
   parsley
2 T. minced onion

1 T. dry sherry
1 t. salt
1/4 t. white pepper

Rinse mushrooms and place in center of sheet of foil. Sprinkle with remaining ingredients. Bring edges of foil up over mushroom mixture and crimp to seal. Set in baking pan and bake at 350° for 30 minutes. Serves 2 to 4.

SPICY CARROTS

"The recipe I really wanted you to include here was for goat cheese and sun-dried tomatoes wrapped in grape leaves. However, I'm remodeling my kitchen and can't find my box of special recipes. I remember that you wrap small pieces of cheese and one-half tomato in each grape leaf, brush with oil and place on a barbecue. (Can also bake or broil in oven.) Yummy! These spicy carrots are just as delicious." Babette Schiller

1 medium onion, sliced thin and separated (1 cup)
8 carrots sliced lengthwise into 1/8" strips (2 cups)
1 large tomato, peeled and chopped
3 T. butter (margarine)
1/2 t. salt
1/8 t. cayenne pepper
1/4 cup finely chopped scallions, including 2" greens
2 T. chopped parsley

Melt butter (margarine) in heavy 12" skillet on high heat. Drop in onion rings and stir frequently. Cook 8-10 minutes on moderate heat until golden. Add tomato and raise heat. Boil briskly, uncovered, until most liquid has evaporated. Add carrots, salt and pepper. Pour in water (1/2 cup) to barely cover carrots. Bring to boil and cover skillet. Reduce heat and simmer 10 minutes until carrots are tender. Place in heated dish and sprinkle with scallions and parsley.

CHAPTER V

KUGELS GALORE

Kugel has entered the vernacular and is so popular a dish that we forget its Eastern European origin. *Kugel* (if you're of Litvak descent, not *Kigel*, and definitely not "pudding") was the official dessert on *Shabbat* after *cholent* was served. It could be baked along with the *cholent* or inside it! Originally prepared with *lokshen* (noodles), *kugel* may today consist of potatoes, rice, or *hallah* and be dairy or meat. It's impossible to fail at making a *kugel*. Use a little imagination and creativity -- and enjoy.

Do not give yourself over to sorrow or distress yourself deliberately.

> A merry heart keeps one alive, and joy lengthens one's days....

> Envy and anger shorten one's life, and anxiety brings premature old age.

> A person with a gay heart has a good appetite and relishes the food he eats.

-Wisdom of Ben Sira, ch. 30, verses 21-22 and 24-25

- Potato
- Cherry Noodle
- Broccoli
- Pecan Pie
- Three-Color
- Bloch's Noodle
- *Sukkah Kugel*
- *Hallah*
- Sweet Potato
- *Matzah* (2)
- Basic Dairy (3)
- Sour Cream Noodle
- Mixed Vegetable
- Zucchini
- Squash

UNIQUE POTATO SALAD

Boil potatoes in their jackets. When done, peel and cut them in squares; while still hot, put on a tablespoonful of butter or drippings of poultry, and add two or more hard-boiled eggs, cut into squares; sprinkle salt and pepper over potatoes and eggs. You may add an onion if you like the flavor. Boil enough vinegar to just cover the salad and add two teaspoonfuls of prepared mustard; beat up the yolks of one or two eggs, and add the boiling vinegar gradually. When thoroughly mixed, pour over the potatoes. Serve in a salad bowl; garnish with chopped parsley. Eat cold.

Aunt Babette

THE *KUGELMAHER'S* FAMOUS
POTATO *KUGEL* (*Parve*)

Some people retire and don't know what to do. Isaac Herstic became famous throughout Westchester for his mouth-watering, delectable potato *kugels*. He made twenty 9"x13" *kugels* for *Shabbos* dinner at our *shul*, grating 100 lbs. of fresh Idaho potatoes in record-breaking time. He whips up a *kugel* if it's your birthday, your anniversary, your child's birthday, if someone's coming to visit, or for any *simhah* at all. And, when you're the *Kugelmaher's rebbetzin*, don't ask. If one of us even looks like we're thinking about his potato *kugel* (or *latkes*), it miraculously appears at the front door, wrapped in foil and a brown paper bag and covered with a nice plastic wrap.

Isaac the *Kugelmaher* always wears a smile, a big white chef's hat and fancy red apron that reads, "The *Kugel* King." The *Kugelmaher* is a loving husband, father and grandfather and one of the most generous, beautiful people we've ever known. May he live to 120 and continue *kugel*-making!

This is the first time Isaac has shared his secret recipe. He says it's been kept in a vault in Rumania for centuries.

Isaac's Instructions:
"First lay out the following items so you shouldn't have to look around for anything."

1 potato peeler -- Isaac prefers a narrow, rubber-grip type
1 grater -- the rectangular lay-across-the-bowl type
1 small saucepan

1 large pot filled with ice cold water
1 large mixing spoon
1 white cotton glove
1 small bowl
1 metal colander
9" x 13" baking pan

Ingredients:
8-10 large Idaho potatoes
1 jumbo egg for every 2 potatoes

1 cup vegetable oil
1 heaping T. salt
3/4 T. pepper

To keep the potatoes from turning black once they are peeled, you must work very quickly. Preheat oven to 250°. Measure one cup oil and pour into saucepan to heat on lowest setting. Peel potatoes and place immediately into a pot of cold water. Break 5 eggs into a bowl and set aside. Wash potatoes with cold water and grate into a large pot.

To grate: Lay grater across top of pot and push against the wall (protect wall with a sponge), anchor your left elbow to a towel and grasp the grater's handle with your left hand. Wearing a white glove on your right hand, select a potato and begin grating back and forth very quickly. When only a small stub remains, place the next potato on top of it and continue grating until all potatoes are grated. Strain water off grated potatoes by pouring into a colander. Turn oil to high until it boils, then turn off the burner. Add eggs, salt and pepper to grated potatoes and mix thoroughly. Pour approximately one-third of the oil into a

---

9"x13" baking pan (Isaac prefers disposable foil baking pans for gifts) and remainder of oil into the *kugel* and mix thoroughly. (The *kugel* begins cooking before your eyes.) Pour mixture into the baking pan and place in center rack of oven for one hour at 350°. Check after one hour. If the *kugel* is not yet brown, shut off oven but leave *kugel* inside until all liquid has been absorbed and *kugel* is totally golden brown.

This is the richest, most delicious potato *kugel* you can imagine, but it will never taste as good as when Isaac the *Kugelmaher* makes it himself!

CHERRY NOODLE *KUGEL*

This recipe comes from Joanne Kaufman.

1 lb. noodles, cooked
1 6-oz. can pineapple
  juice
4 eggs, lightly beaten
1 t. vanilla
4 T. margarine

3/4 cup brown sugar
1 can cherry (or other)
  pie filling
Corn flake crumbs,
  mixed with sugar
  and cinnamon

Mix eggs, pineapple, vanilla, sugar and melted margarine in with noodles. Pour 1/2 of noodle mixture into the bottom of a 9"x13" pan. Cover with cherry pie filling. Pour the remainder of the noodle mixture on top of the layer of pie filling. Sprinkle with corn flake crumbs that have been combined with sugar and cinnamon. Bake at 350° for 1 to 1 1/4 hours. Serves 10-12.

BETE'S BROCCOLI *KUGEL (Parve)*

This is delicious and easy to take along for gourmet picnics.

2 packages frozen
  chopped broccoli
3 eggs (beaten)
1/2 cup mayonnaise

1/2 cup water
3 T. onion soup mix
1 1/2 T. margarine
1 1/2 T. flour

Mix all ingredients and fold in beaten eggs. Place in greased 9"x12" pyrex or disposable foil pan and bake at 400° for 45 minutes. Serves 6.

PECAN *KUGEL* "PIE" (Dairy or *Parve*)

Never make less than two of these. It's like eating candy -- you just can't stop!

Crust:

1/4 cup butter or *parve* margarine (melted)
1/2 cup brown sugar

1 cup pecans (chopped)

Pour shortening into 6-cup casserole. Spread with sugar and sprinkle with pecans and set aside.

Filling:

1 8-oz. package medium noodles
2 T. butter or *parve* margarine (melted)
2 eggs (beaten)
1/4 cup light raisins

8 dried apricots (chopped)
1 apple (peeled, thinly sliced)
1/4 cup sugar
1/4 t. cinnamon

Boil noodles in 2 1/2 quarts salted water for 10 minutes. Rinse with hot water and drain. Toss with shortening. Combine remaining ingredients and mix well. Place in refrigerator for 2 hours, then spread onto prepared crust. Sprinkle with topping and bake 1 1/2 hours at 350°. Serves 6-8.

Topping:

1/4 cup corn flake crumbs

2 T. butter or *parve* margarine

Melt shortening in saucepan. Add corn flakes and mix well.

THREE-COLOR *KUGEL* (*Parve*)

This delicious *kugel* is another work of art created by Ceil Skydell.

You will need to make 3 batches of the mixture listed below. To the first batch, add cooked broccoli and process in blender. Spoon into a pretty bowl or dish and freeze.

To the second batch, add cooked carrots (which have cooled) and process in blender. Remove dish from freezer and spoon blended carrot mixture on top of broccoli layer and return dish to freezer.

To the third batch, add cooked cauliflower (cooled) and process in blender. Remove dish from freezer and spoon blended cauliflower on top of carrot layer.

Mixture (Make 3 batches)
2 eggs   1/4 cup mayonnaise
1 1/2 T. oil   3 T. liquid *parve*
1 1/2 T. flour   creamer

Vegetables
Broccoli (16 oz.   Cauliflower (16 oz.
  frozen), cooked   frozen), cooked
Carrots (16 oz. frozen),
  cooked

Sprinkle corn flake crumbs on top and bake at 350° for 1 1/4 hours. Serves 6.

STELLA BLOCH'S NOODLE *KUGEL* (Dairy)

Just as Mrs. Maccabbee kept Judah and his brothers well fed with *latkes*, so Stella Bloch sustained all the Bloch men (and women!) with her famous sweet dairy pudding.

1/2 lb. bag Penn Dutch
   noodles
4 eggs, beaten slightly
1/2 cup sugar
1/2 cup milk
2 apples, peeled &
   chopped, not too fine

1 T. vanilla
1/2 cup water
1/2 cup cottage cheese
1/2 pint sour cream
small can crushed
   pineapple
raisins, as you like

Boil and drain noodles. Do not rinse. Mix in the other ingredients. Pour into a greased square baking pan.

Topping:
1/4 lb. melted butter
1/2 cup crushed
   corn flake crumbs
1/2 t. cinnamon

1 T. sugar
1/2 jar apricot butter
   or jam (optional)

Mix first four ingredients together and spread over top of pudding. Drop apricot butter on top. Bake one hour at 350°. Serves 1-8.

THE "RUNNING OF THE NOODLES"
As told by Dr. Shulamith Elster of Rockville, Maryland

We arrived in Youngstown, Ohio, in April of 1964 with a six-month-old daughter, Elana, and a twenty-one-month-old-son, Jonathan. Both had been born while my husband, Rabbi Shelly, served for two years as an Army Chaplain at Fort Lee, Virginia. Congregation Ohev Tzedek was to be his first civilian pulpit and community. We lived there until 1968 and then moved East to Alexandria with a third child, Adam.

The "rabbinage" was a lovely but small house on an enormous piece of land close to the synagogue. We filled the house -- to say the least. *Yom Tov* came late that year and although people had warned us about the Youngstown and Ohio winters, we were not prepared for the cold weather to arrive (what we thought was) so soon. Anxious to be the model of proper etiquette, we invited the congregation for *kiddush* in our *Sukkah* on the second day of *Sukkot*. It got very cold several days before and I thought that there would be no way to keep people (about whom we cared) outdoors in that cold. HELP!

I called home and sought the advice of a most experienced hostess, my mother. She suggested that given the size of the house and the wall-to-wall children's decor, we find a way to keep everyone out-of-doors and warm. She gave me a recipe that had been given to her by her cousin Lena Machlis Berger (z'l), who had received it from a friend, Dora Gaba, who had edited a cookbook for her Sisterhood at the Garden City Jewish Center somewhere in the late '60s. Somewhere I have a copy of the cookbook.

The *kiddush* was a great success. I served all of the usual *kiddush* items, very HOT coffee and HOT *kugel* -- which we came to call the "In The *Sukkah Kugel*." I enjoyed the rave reviews for the *kugel* and thought no more about it. One *Shabbat* after services the following summer -- it was mid-August with temperatures too hot to handle -- one of the elderly gentlemen (you know the gentlemen to whom I refer -- the backbone of the *minyan* in small towns all over the United States... long may they live...) informed me that there were only some eight weeks until *Sukkot*. He was waiting for his next piece of *kugel*.

We served the *kugel* for the next four years in Youngstown and then for some sixteen of the nineteen years we lived in Alexandria. One year I tried to substitute *blintzes*, but everyone wanted the *kugel*! Another year I tried again with *pirogen*...but clearly it was the "In The *Sukkah Kugel*" that hit the spot and was our *Sukkot* tradition.

This *Sukkot* will be the 31st anniversary of what I call the "running of the noodles." Imagine the looks I got when ingredients of a *kugel* for over 100 people were piled onto the check-out counter at the market!

Come For Everything ... But *Cholent*   103

SHULAMITH'S "IN THE *SUKKAH KUGEL*"

1 lb. medium OR wide noodles (I prefer the wide ones)
1 pint sour cream
1 cup sugar (hold back 5 T.)
1/2 lb. melted butter (hold back 5 T.)
3/4 lbs. cream cheese
2 cups corn flakes
6 eggs
juice & rind of a lemon

Cook noodles and drain. Beat eggs and then add sugar, melted butter, the mashed cream cheese, lemon rind and juice and sour cream. Add to noodles.

Topping:
Crumble corn flakes and add melted butter and sugar that were reserved. Spread on top.

Use a buttered or greased large oblong baking dish (Pyrex is fine), or you can use casserole dishes for the *kugel*. Pour mixture in and spread topping. Cover with aluminum foil. Refrigerate overnight.

Before baking in a 350° oven, remove the foil. Bake for an hour. It can be frozen after baking.

This *kugel* serves 8 large portions (or 12 medium). To extend this *kugel* recipe, the noodles can be doubled and the other ingredients remain as written. (Not quite as rich but still tasty and delicious.) Also, low-fat ingredients can be substituted. The basic recipe is so rich that it's sinful.

<u>H</u>ALLAH LEFTOVERS *KUGEL* (*Parve*)

It's often a debate in our home as to whether leftover <u>h</u>allah should be used for making Sunday morning French toast or this delicious *kugel* for supper.

1 1/2 lbs. <u>h</u>allah (whole or pieces)	1 lb. mushrooms, sliced
water	5 eggs
1 onion, minced	salt & pepper, to taste
1/3 cup oil	Italian spices

Soak <u>h</u>allah in water to cover for a minute or two and squeeze out excess. Fry onion and mushrooms in oil. Beat eggs and mix all ingredients. Grease 9"x12" baking pan and bake for one hour at 325°. Serves 8.

SWEET POTATO *KUGELA<u>H</u>* (*Parve*)

These small *kugels* are great for party buffets as well as *Shabbat* dinners or any time.

3 cups mashed sweet potatoes	1/4 cup honey
3-4 T. oil	1 cup water
3 eggs	1 t. salt
1/2 cup brown sugar	rind and juice of 1 lemon
1 t. ginger	

Mix all ingredients and spoon into greased muffin tins, two-thirds full. Bake at 350° for 30 minutes. Serves 6 to 8.

MATZAH KUGELS FOR PASSOVER

They're both sweet and delicious.

KUGEL #1 (*Parve*)

12 complete pieces of
  matzah
9 eggs, well beaten
1/2 t. salt
1 1/2 cups sugar
3/4 cup oil

3 t. cinnamon
1 1/2 cups chopped
  walnuts
6 large apples, cored,
  peeled and sliced
1 1/2 cups raisins

Break *matzah* into pieces and soak in water until soft. Drain. Beat eggs with salt, sugar, oil and cinnamon. Add to drained *matzah* and stir in nuts, apples and raisins. Pour into large roasting pan. Bake in 350° pre-heated oven for 50 minutes. Serves 12 or more.

KUGEL #2 (*Parve*)

3 cups *matzah farfel*
5 eggs, separated
1/2 T. salt
4 T. sugar
1 T. cinnamon
2 cups apple sauce

1 stick melted
  margarine
1 small can crushed
  pineapple (drained)
cinnamon/sugar
  mixture

Pour hot water over *farfel* in colander. Beat together yolks, salt, sugar and margarine and mix with *farfel*. Add fruit and cinnamon. Fold in stiff egg whites. Pour into 9"x13" pan. Top with cinnamon/sugar. Bake at 350° for 30-45 minutes. Serves 8-10.

BASIC DAIRY NOODLE *KUGEL*

Down to basics and then some variations on the "theme."

1/2 lb. broad noodles (cooked)	1/4 cup butter (melted)
3 eggs (well beaten)	1 t. salt
1 lb. cottage cheese	1/2 cup raisins
1 t. cinnamon	1/2 cup sugar

Mix all ingredients thoroughly. Pour into greased 2-quart baking dish. Bake at 350° for one hour. Serves 4-6.

Variation 1: Pineapple *Kugel*

1/2 lb. medium noodles (cook, drain dry)	pinch of salt
	1/2 lb. cottage cheese
3 eggs	1 cup raisins
2 cups milk	1 apple (diced)
1/2 cup sugar	small can crushed pineapple
1 t. vanilla	

Mix all ingredients thoroughly. In a 12" square pan, melt 1/2 lb. butter, then add mixture. Sprinkle sugar and cinnamon on top. Bake for an hour at 350°.

Variation 2: Coconut *Kugel*

1/2 lb. broad noodles
4 eggs
1/2 t. salt
1 stick margarine
5 T. sugar
3 t. vanilla

1 pint sour cream
1/2 cup raisins
1/4 cup coconut
1/2 cup sugar
corn flakes

Cook noodles and drain thoroughly. Combine eggs, salt, sugar, vanilla, sour cream and raisins. Melt the margarine and stir half of it into the egg mixture. Pour the remaining margarine into a 3-quart shallow baking dish. Bake for 40 minutes at 350°. Crumble coconut and cereal on top and return to oven for 10 more minutes.

Variation 3: Fruited *Kugel*

1 lb. broad noodles
1 1/2 pint sour cream
1 1/2 cup butter
   (melted)
1 1/2 cup sugar
1 t. vanilla
5 eggs (beaten)

2 cans (6 oz.) crushed
   pineapple
1 package dried apple
   slices
1 package dried
   apricots

Cook noodles and drain. Grease large pan. Place a layer of dried apple slices on bottom. Pour in rest of ingredients and sprinkle top with cinnamon and sugar. Bake 45 minutes at 350°. Serves 10.

SOUR CREAM NOODLE *KUGEL*

Elaine Bieber says this recipe is her family's favorite. Try it. It might become yours!

12 oz. broad noodles, boiled
5 eggs
2 t. vanilla

1 lb. cottage cheese
8 oz. sour cream
1 cup sugar

Topping:
1 stick butter
3 T. sugar

1 1/2 cups cookie or *kichel* crumbs

Mix eggs, vanilla and sugar. Add noodles, cottage cheese and sour cream. Fold. Add crumb mixture (topping). Bake in 9"x12" aluminum foil tin or other pan for 40 minutes at 350°. Serves 8-10.

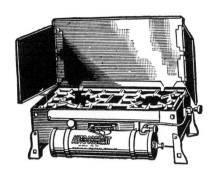

VEGETABLE *KUGELS*

For a change of pace, forget the noodles.

•MIXED VEGETABLE *KUGEL* (*Parve*)

1 lb. squash, peeled
2 large carrots, peeled
2 large potatoes,
  peeled
1 large onion

2 eggs
2 slices bread, any kind
salt & pepper, to taste
bread crumbs

Grate or process the raw vegetables and bread. Drain off some liquid if batter is watery. Add eggs, salt and pepper. Mix thoroughly. Add bread crumbs if mixture seems too loose. Bake in oblong greased pan at 350° for one hour or until brown. Serves 8 or more.

•ZUCCHINI SOUFFLE (*Parve*)

2 lbs. zucchini, peeled
2 eggs
2 T. flour

1 T. oil
salt & pepper, to taste

Cook zucchini and mash. Add to well-beaten eggs and mix well together with flour, oil, salt and pepper. Placed in greased baking dish and bake in 350° oven for 30 minutes. Serves 6 to 8.

•SQUASH SOUFFLE (Dairy)

4 squash, grated
5 eggs, separated
2 T. water

1 package dry
   mushroom soup mix
1 cup skim milk

With electric mixer, whip egg whites together with water. Add yolks and fold in grated squash. Add mushroom soup mix and milk. Pour into greased baking dish and bake in 350° oven 40-45 minutes. If desired, sprinkle some yellow grated cheese on top and bake 3-5 minutes longer. Serves 6.

•APPLE *KUGEL* (*Parve*)

4 red apples
4 eggs, separated
1/2 cup *matzah* meal
1/2 cup white raisins

1/2 cup imitation
   sugar
juice of 1/2 lemon

Peel and grate apples. Beat egg yolks with sugar until light in color. Add lemon juice, apples and *matzah* meal. Add raisins. Beat egg whites until stiff and fold into mixture. Pour into greased baking dish and bake at 325° for approximately 40 minutes.

Do not sit too much, for sitting aggravates hemor-rhoids;

Do not stand too much, for standing hurts the heart;

Do not walk too much, for walking hurts the eyes.

So, spend one third of your time sitting, one third standing, and one third walking.

Babylonian Talmud, tractate
Ketubbot, page 111a

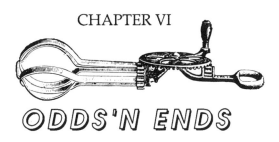

CHAPTER VI

ODDS'N ENDS

Our tradition mixes superstition and folk remedies with practical advice to teach a simple lesson: Eat wisely.

13 things were said concerning eating bread in the morning:

> It protects against heat and cold, winds and demons.
> It makes the simple wise, causes a person to win lawsuits, and helps a person to study and teach Torah, to have his words heeded, and to retain scholarship.
> A person who eats in the morning doesn't exhale a bad odor and lives with his wife without lusting after other women.
> Morning bread also kills the worms in a person's intestines.
> And some people say it gets rid of jealousy and encourages love....
> A proverb says: "Sixty runners speed along but cannot overtake the person who breaks bread in the morning."

> *-Babylonia Talmud, tractate*
> *Bava Mezia, page 107b*

- A Pink Tea
- Black Radish Preserves
- *Haroset*
- Oil 'n Onions
- Mulled Wine
- Mulled Cider
- Sangria
- Champagne Punch
- Carrot *Tzimmes* with *Knaidel*
- Sweet Potato and Prune *Tzimmes*
- Sweet Potato and Apple *Tzimmes*
- Candy
- Baked Apples
- Caramelized Apples

Talk not while you eat lest windpipe anticipate gullet (and life be in danger).

Talmud, Ta'anit

A PINK TEA
from *Aunt Babette's Cookbook*

"Pink Teas, just now so fashionable, are rather novel if carried out to the letter, and an expensive way of entertaining, too; yet, as the old saying is, one might as well be dead as out of fashion. So all those who wish to be fashionable come and listen, and I will give you a few hints in regard to getting up a "Pink Tea." As a matter of course, the table linen should be pink; the dishes also of a delicate pink shade, which you may borrow for the occasion. Arrange white cakes on high cake-stands, lined with fancy pink paper, or pink napkins, and put pink frosted cakes on low cake-stands lined with fancy white paper or napkins. The flowers for decoration must also be of pink. Serve the creams and ices in novel designs made of pink paper, such as baskets, boxes, buckets, freezers, cups and saucers, shells, wheelbarrows, vases, etc. I am not able to tell you all the different designs they have for this purpose. You may procure these and many more beautiful designs at almost any fashionable caterer's. Each guest should have a pink boutonniere, or a white hyacinth, tied with a pink satin ribbon. Have miniature fans placed for each guest, with a card attached containing his or her name; these are to be taken home as souvenirs. Serve the butter in pink individuals, each piece of butter molded differently and garnished with a wreath of parsley. A handsome center-piece for the table is indispensable, so get a large fruit-stand and trim it prettily with ferns, smilax and flowers, or have an ornament of spun sugar for a center-piece. If you live where there are no caterers, you may try this: make a large nest of macaroons, oval in shape, join the macaroons with sugar boiled until it candies; have this

---

filled with charlotte russe and resting on a rock of spun sugar. You may color the charlotte russe pink; the effect will be beautiful, for the spun sugar will look like crystal. A nice way to serve charlottes at a "Pink Tea" is to hollow out large "Acme" tomatoes, skin them carefully, cut off the tops and scoop out the inside, set on ice until wanted, then fill with whipped cream and ornament with candied cherries. (At a "Yellow Tea" you may substitute oranges for this purpose.) Your waitresses should wear a pink cap and a pink apron. Illuminate the table with pink "fairy lamps" or a chandelier or candles."

BLACK RADISH *EINGEMAHTS*
(PRESERVES)

Eingemahts are preserves. Those made from vegetables were ingeniously devised long ago when
fruits were not plentiful. Beets, black radishes and
carrots were most frequently used. On *Pesah*, my
mother, of blessed memory, used to serve beet or
black radish *eingemahts* in pretty white dishes
decorated with mallard ducks. The beets were
taken from russell borscht fermenting in a crock for
many weeks, so forget that recipe. I don't remember the recipe for carrots, but here's the black
radish variety. Later on, mom switched to purple
plums -- what a treat!

4 cups black radishes, cut in strips	2 t. ginger, ground
3 cups sugar	1/2 cup cold water
1 cup honey	1 cup almonds, sliced

Scrub radishes, pare and slice. Parboil in water to
cover for 10 minutes. Drain, repeat again and
drain again. In a large saucepan, cook honey,
sugar, ginger and water until it becomes syrupy.
Add radish strips and cook until they begin to look
translucent. Add nuts and simmer until it thickens
to jam consistency. This may be stored in the
refrigerator or preserved in jelly glasses. This
recipe makes approximately 6-8 eight-ounce containers.

_H_AROSET A LA BILL DANTZIC

Bill, a Baltimore Hebrew College classmate of my husband's, showed up for our _seder_ a few years ago and forever changed our taste for _Pesa_h _h_aroset.

2 large bananas
2 large Valencia (juice)
  oranges
16 oz. walnut pieces,
  unsalted
12 oz. pitted dates,
  unsugared

36 small figs, stems
  removed
cinnamon, to taste
sweet Concord grape
  wine, to taste and to
  moisten mixture

All ingredients should be ground or mashed thoroughly. It is strongly recommended that you use a food processor -- otherwise, you will spend a week with a mortar and chopping bowl and end up with a very sore shoulder and callouses on your hand!

Make sure the seeds and as much membrane as possible are removed from the oranges. (I find that grinding the dates and figs with some orange or banana keeps the former from wadding up into a big ball in the processor.)

Combine all the ground ingredients in a large bowl, add cinnamon to taste and use the Concord wine to moisten. Remember to add a little bit (1/2 cup) of wine at a time. Then let it sit 15 minutes. The ground nuts will absorb the wine at first so, after time, you may have to add more. Never worry -- you're going to have 4 cups of wine at the _seder_ anyway.

Don't be surprised at the volume of _haroset_ this makes. It is guaranteed to disappear at an alarming rate. If you are going to someone else's _seder_, this makes a wonderful gift to take if you don't mind embarrassing your host and hostess when their _haroset_ is passed up in favor of yours.

INSTANT _HAROSET_

One year, as our _seder_ guests were arriving, I realized I hadn't prepared our family's traditional _haroset_ recipe of grated apples, walnuts, wine and ginger. I quickly improvised by taking a jar of Passover applesauce and added the other ingredients. Everyone loved it.

2 cups applesauce
1 12-oz. package
   chopped walnuts
1 T. powdered ginger

sweet red wine, as
   needed
1 t. powdered
   cinnamon

Mix all ingredients to desired consistency. Store in glass jar in refrigerator.

OUR SECRET INGREDIENT --
MOCK *SHMALTZ*

By now it's probably known world-wide that the secret ingredient needed in Kosher cuisine is fried onions. They lend a *yiddishe ta'am* -- a certain Jewish flavor -- delicious and familiar. My mother's refrigerator always held a jar of golden *shmaltz* while mine generally holds a jar of fried onions in oil. It doesn't take much...a half teaspoon here, a half there.... Sheer ambrosia.

Finely mince 1 sweet onion. Place in a heavy saucepan and cover with 1/2 cup oil. (Use a *parve* pan so oil and onions can be added to meat <u>or</u> dairy dishes.) Slowly simmer until onions turn almost golden. (The secret is to remove from stove before they turn golden as they will continue to cook in the hot oil.) Allow to cool and store in glass jar in the refrigerator.

Add a bit to chopped eggs and onions, chopped eggplant, chopped liver, or mock liver spreads, mashed potatoes, kasha, lentils, beans and, of course, to your *cholent* pot. (Oops, there I go again!)

PARTY PUNCH

Hot or cold, for festive, gracious entertaining.

MULLED WINE

2 bottles (fifths)
  burgundy or sherry
1 orange, unpeeled,
  sliced
2 lemons, unpeeled,
  sliced

3/4 cup sugar
3 sticks cinnamon
1 t. allspice
20 cloves, whole
1/2 cup fresh lemon
  juice

Place all ingredients in a slow-cooker. Stir to mix well. Cover pot. Cook on low for 4 hours, or on high, 2 hours. Serve hot.

MULLED CIDER

2 quarts apple cider
1/2 cup brown sugar
2 sticks cinnamon
1 1/2 t. cloves, whole

1 t. allspice, whole
2 oranges, unpeeled,
  sliced

In a cheesecloth bag, tie the cinnamon, cloves and allspice. Place all ingredients in a pot and simmer for one hour. Remove spice bag. Serve hot.

SANGRIA SUPREME

While living in Mexico City, we often served sangria -- a drink of equal parts red wine and lemonade. Here's a newer, lighter version we enjoy serving.

1 cup red grape juice
2 T. lime juice
2 T. orange juice
1 T. lemon juice
1 cup club soda

Combine all ingredients and serve over ice. Fresh orange slices may be added for garnish. Serves 2.

CHAMPAGNE PUNCH

For a large punch bowl (about 2 gallons).

1 16-oz. can frozen
  pineapple juice
1 16-oz. can frozen
  orange juice
2 16-oz. cans water
strawberry & orange
  slices
1 bottle champagne
1 2-liter bottle ginger
  ale

For ice ring:
Make the ice ring in advance. Use a ring mold pan (or bowl) and fill with water. Arrange orange slices and strawberries in water and freeze until solid.

For punch:
Mix all ingredients, adding champagne and ginger ale immediately prior to serving. Run hot water over ice ring to loosen and slide into punch bowl.

SUCH A *TZIMMES*

Tzimmes has made it into the dictionary as "a fuss or tumult." In cooking, a *tzimmes* may be almost any combination of meat with fruits or vegetables, or even fruits or vegetables without meat. That's probably why I love *tzimmes* almost as much as *cholent* -- you throw it together and it always tastes delicious. In cooking any *tzimmes*, like *cholent*, it is important that it be cooked slowly for a long time to get the best blending of flavors. Generally, when we say *tzimmes* we think of sweet *mehren tzimmes* -- carrots sliced in rounds with a few prunes and a roux of flour, oil and seasonings added at the end of cooking. *Tzimmes* is often served on *Rosh Hashanah* because it is a sweet dish and symbolic of the wish for a year of sweetness. The fact that it can be prepared in advance and kept warm also makes it a good *Shabbat* and holiday dish.

CARROT *TZIMMES* WITH *KNAIDEL*

Mehren (carrot) *tzimmes* is one of our favorites.

1 lb. brisket
boiling water to cover
3 sweet potatoes,
   peeled and quartered
6 carrots, peeled and
   cut in rounds

1 medium onion, sliced
3 T. honey
2 T. flour
ginger, salt & pepper,
   to taste

Cover the meat with water, season and simmer for one hour. Remove meat to a 3-quart casserole, saving liquid. Arrange vegetables around the meat and cover with liquid. Stir in the honey. Bake at 350° for one hour. Mix flour, ginger and salt and pepper with a little broth to make a *roux* (a thin paste). Stir into casserole and mix thoroughly. Return to oven and prepare *knaidel*.

Knaidel recipe
1 cup flour
1 t. baking power
1/2 cup vegetable or
   peanut oil

1 T. minced onion
1 T. minced parsley
salt & pepper, to taste
2 or 3 T. water

Mix dry ingredients and add oil, onion and parsley. Stir in water, a little at a time, to make a ball of dough.

Clear a spot in the casserole to insert *knaidel* (one large ball of dough). Then cover and bake at 200° for 50-60 minutes. Uncover and brown. Serves 6.

SWEET POTATO AND PRUNE *TZIMMES*

Traditional style.

1 1/2 lbs. prunes
1 onion, chopped
3 lbs. brisket or flanken
   (optional)
5 medium sweet
   potatoes, cut in
   coarse pieces

3 cups boiling water
2 T. oil
1/3 cup brown sugar
   or 1/2 cup honey
cinnamon, salt &
   pepper, to taste

Wash the prunes and soak in boiling water. Heat the oil in a large, heavy saucepan. Cut the meat into chunks and brown with the onion. Sprinkle with salt and pepper, cover pan and cook over low heat for one hour. Add the prunes and the water in which they were soaked, the sweet potatoes, sugar or honey and cinnamon. Replace the cover loosely and cook over low heat for several hours or place it in a casserole and bake at 350° until the meat is tender. Serves 6-8.

Can be made with carrots instead of potatoes.

SWEET POTATO AND APPLE *TZIMMES*

A health-conscious variation.

1 1/4 lbs. sweet potatoes	2 T. cornstarch
1/2 cup water	3 T. water
1 lb. apples	1/2 cup honey
1 cup apple juice	1/3 cup wheat germ

In a pot with a tight-fitting lid, steam sweet potatoes in 1/2 cup water until tender (15-20 minutes). Peel and slice lengthwise in 1/2" thick slices. Layer in casserole.

Peel and core apples, slicing them 1/2" thick. Lay apple slices on top of sweet potatoes.

Heat apple juice to boiling. Combine cornstarch and water and add to juice, cooking until the sauce is clear and thickened. Add honey.

Spoon sauce over apples, then top with wheat germ. Bake at 350° until apples are tender (approximately an hour). Serves 6.

POMERANTZEN (candied citrus peel)

How could a Pomerantz resist these delectable *pomerantzen*?

the peel of 6 large
  oranges
1 lb. 5 oz. sugar

1 1/2 cups water
juice of 1 lemon

Wash the fruit and remove the peel in sections. Cut into narrow strips. Cover with water and bring to a boil. Change water and repeat entire process 5 times. Drain. Mix the sugar and water until syrupy and add to the peels. When all the liquid has been absorbed, add the juice of one lemon and stir. Drain and roll the strips of peel in some sugar. Allow to dry on a rack for a day or two until dry.

BAKED APPLES

Who doesn't love a baked apple!

4 apples   cinnamon and sugar,
                              to taste.

Wash apples and core, leaving them whole. Place in microwaveable 1" deep dish. Sprinkle the centers with cinnamon and sugar and microwave for 4 minutes or until tender. For variety, add butter and chopped walnuts or drizzle with honey and orange juice. Serves 4.

CARAMELIZED APPLES

A lovely dessert.

2 Granny Smith apples   1 T. brown sugar
2 T. butter

Peel, core and slice apples. Place everything in a non-stick skillet over medium-low heat and cook until tender. Stir and turn apple slices as juices begin to caramelize (about 10 minutes). Serve warm. Serves 4.

CHAPTER VII

ODDS 'N ENDS IN
5 MINUTES OR LESS

Five things were said of garlic:

> It satisfies your hunger.
> It keeps the body warm.
> It makes your face bright.
> It increases a man's potency.
> It kills parasites in the bowels.

Some people say that it also encourages love and removes jealousy.

-Babylonian Talmud, tractate Bava Kamma

- Instant Burgers
- Grilled Cheese and Artichoke Sandwiches
- Cucumber Cups
- Cucumber Salad
- Low-Fat Spanish Rice
- Beet Horseradish
- Beer Batter
- Pickled Peppers
- Italian *Salsa Verde*
- Infused Oils
- Raspberry Sauce
- Spiced Pomegranate Syrup
- Date Apple Syrup
- Apricot-Fig Syrup
- Russian Tea
- Mock Orange Julius
- Chocolate *Matzahs*
- Strawberry Whip

GRIMSLICH

Half a loaf of bread, which has been soaked and pressed; four eggs, one cup of sugar, raisins, cinnamon, almonds pounded fine; beat whites to a froth and add last. Fry in hot fat.

Aunt Babette

"INSTANT" BURGERS

My mother-in-law, Jennie Zelonky Pomerantz, taught Hebrew School every day from 4-6 PM and rushed home to feed her family of five. This forced her to either plan ahead or devise "instant" dinners. Her son showed me how to make her instant "burgers" in less than 5 minutes.

1 package *parve* sandwich bread	seasoned salt or any desired combination of spices
1/2 lb ground hamburger meat[*]	

Line a cookie tray with foil. Place bread slices on tray. Pre-heat broiler while thinly spreading meat on bread. Be sure to spread evenly all the way to bread crust. Sprinkle lightly with seasoning and broil until lightly brown and before crust starts to burn. The meat "melts" into the bread and is delicious. Serve with sliced vegetables and fresh fruit for an "instant" dinner. Serves a small army!

[*]Ground chicken or turkey may be substituted.

GRILLED CHEESE AND ARTICHOKE SANDWICHES

This sandwich packs nicely for picnics, chasing butterflies and running barefoot on the grass. It's also possible to enjoy at your desk or at the kitchen table.

4 sandwich rolls, split
8 non-fat cheese slices
1 cup artichoke hearts, cooked and sliced

8 thin tomato slices
2 t. mustard (your choice)
2 T. oil-free Italian dressing

Spread mustard on top half of each sandwich roll. Place bottom halves on foil-covered baking sheet. Top each half with 2 slices of cheese, 1/4 cup of the sliced artichoke hearts and 2 tomato slices. Drizzle each with a small amount of the Italian dressing. Broil 2 minutes or until cheese melts. Cover with tops and serve or roll in foil for later picnic travel. Serves 4.

CUCUMBER CUPS

We attended a fancy Long Island wedding where vodka was served in carved cucumber "cups." I came home inspired to create an interesting appetizer -- stuffed cucumber cups.

2 long and firm cucumbers

Run fork tines down all sides of each cucumber. Trim ends and cut cucumber into thirds. Scoop out seeds being careful to leave a base at the bottom of each "cup." Fill cups with your favorite appetizer or side-dish. My favorite so far is a cucumber cup filled with minty tabouli. Serve by placing cup on top a bed of lettuce, endive and raddiccio. Also try filling cups with salmon salad, chopped herring, chopped eggs or caviar. Serves 6.

CUCUMBER SALAD

This salad is often sold at take-out counters, but it never tastes as good as home-made. And it's so easy to make!

3 cucumbers, thinly sliced	sugar (or imitation sugar), to taste
1 large sweet vidalia onion, thinly sliced	vinegar (or lemon juice), to taste
	salt & pepper, to taste

Mix all ingredients in a bowl. Set a plate on top and put a weight on top of it. (A large food can or sturdy rock will do just fine.) Place in refrigerator and chill one hour or more.

LOW-FAT SPANISH RICE

This low-fat recipe is an easy addition to any meal. It can be put together quickly and is full of flavor.

1 cup uncooked instant rice
1 cup onion, chopped
1/2 cup red pepper, diced
1/2 t. mustard
1/4 t. pepper

1 14-oz. can whole tomatoes, undrained and chopped
1 5-oz. can tomato juice
vegetable cooking spray

Coat a large non-stick skillet with cooking spray and place over medium heat until hot. Add rice, onion and pepper and sauté 5 minutes. Add remaining ingredients and simmer uncovered for 5 minutes or until liquid is absorbed. Serves 3.

BEET HORSERADISH

I remember watching my father, of blessed memory, *riben* (grating) on the back porch *erev Pesaḥ* each year. As I continue that tradition, my tears are both of memory and the distinct essence of fresh horse-radish.

1 cup freshly grated horseradish
1 medium-sized raw beet, finely grated

1 t. sugar
1/2 t. salt
vinegar, as needed

Mix first four ingredients. Stir in vinegar to make proper consistency (similar to applesauce). Bottle tightly. Makes 1/2 pint and stores well.

BEER BATTER

(Perfect for frying chicken, fish or vegetables -- and great for onion rings.)

For that odd occasion when nothing else will satisfy your craving....

1 can beer 1 T. paprika
1 cup flour   1 T. salt

Put beer into a deep bowl. Sift flour into beer. Add salt and paprika and whisk until light and frothy. Heat oil and keep at high temperature while frying.

INSTANT PICKLED PEPPERS

Actually ready as quickly as you can recite "Peter Piper picked a peck of pickled peppers. If Peter Piper picked a peck of pickled peppers, where are the pickled peppers that Peter Piper picked?"

2 sweet red peppers   2 garlic cloves
red wine vinegar, as   salt & pepper, to taste
  needed

Singe peppers on direct flame until they are black all over. (If you have an electric stove, place beneath oven broiler.) Peel and take out seeds and veins. Slice and place in glass bowl.

Chop garlic and place on top of peppers in bowl. Add vinegar to cover, season with salt and pepper. Chill for one hour if you can wait that long!

ITALIAN *SALSA VERDE*

It's green and oh-so-tangy!

1/2 cup parsley,
chopped fine
1/2 cup capers,
chopped
1/2 cup olive oil

1/4 cup scallions,
chopped
2 cloves garlic,
chopped fine
2 T. lemon juice

In a bowl, whisk all ingredients together. Cover and refrigerate. Can be made up to a week in advance. Delicious on salads, fish or chicken.

INFUSED OILS

Infused oils for grilling and broiling are very "in" at the moment. The following recipe can be used for grilling fish or dipping French bread. We also like it on baked potatoes.

2 cups olive oil
3 cloves garlic, crushed
zest of lemon peel

1/4 cup chopped
parsley
1/4 cup chopped basil

Combine all ingredients in a small jar and allow to blend. To avoid contamination, oils should be made in small batches and kept refrigerated and used within a few days.

Come For Everything ... But *Cholent*

RASPBERRY SAUCE

This sauce is delicious on ice cream and waffles.

1 cup fresh raspberries   2 T. Sabra liqueur from
                            Israel

Place raspberries in a blender or food processor
and blend until smooth. Strain through a fine sieve
to remove seeds. Add Sabra and blend well. This
recipe yields one cup.

SPICED POMEGRANATE SYRUP

Shir HaShirim, The Song of Songs, inspires this
recipe: "I would cause them to drink of spiced
wine, of the juice of my pomegranate."

1 cup sugar   1 cup water
1/4 t. nutmeg   pomegranate juice
1/8 t. cinnamon   (fresh or bottled)
1/8 t. ginger   1 lemon, sliced
2 whole cloves

Combine sugar, spices and water and simmer for
5 minutes. Chill. Add pomegranate juice, as
desired. May be diluted with water to taste, or may
be added to tea (hot or iced).

SENSUAL SYRUPS

Great for pouring over sweets or fruit; adding to drinks for flavoring; and spooning on top of frozen yogurts and ice cream.

DATE-APPLE SYRUP

6 dates, pitted
1/2 cup dried apples

3/4 cup seedless grapes

Soak dates and apples in water (just enough to cover) overnight. Put grapes in blender for 5 seconds. Add dates and apples and blend an additional 5 seconds. Add some of soaking water to blender as needed to give you the right consistency (thicker for toppings and creamier for drinks).

APRICOT-FIG SYRUP

1 cup dried apricots

2/3 cup figs

Soak dried apricots and figs overnight in just enough water to cover. Blend in an electric blender with just enough soaking water to purée. Pour over fruits.

INSTANT RUSSIAN TEA

A recipe created by Ruth Bovarnick of Mercer Island, WA. The zest and zip of this drink doesn't begin to describe her vivaciousness and enthusiasm!

2 cups instant orange
  mix
1 1/2 cups sugar
1/2 cup instant tea

1 t. cinnamon
1/2 t. cloves
1 t. allspice

Mix together. Store in jar. Use 2-3 teaspoons per cup of boiling water.

MOCK ORANGE JULIUS

A cool and refreshing drink imitating the commercial creation.

3 oz. orange juice
1/2 cup milk
1/2 cup water
1/8 cup sugar

1/2 t. vanilla
5-6 ice cubes

Combine and blend.

CHOCOLATE *MATZAHS*

Making these *matzahs* is a terrific family activity.

First assemble the following: saucepan or double-boiler, cookie sheet, waxed paper, mixing spoon, rolling pin and measuring spoon.

1 large package chocolate chips (or 12 oz. chopped chocolate bar)	1 T. margarine 4 complete pieces of *matzah*

Melt chocolate and margarine over low heat. Stir to prevent burning. Break *matzah* into pieces and stir into chocolate. Cover a cookie sheet with waxed paper. Pour chocolate *matzah* mixture onto waxed paper and cover with a sheet of waxed paper.

Flatten mixture with rolling pin. Refrigerate. When mixture hardens, peel off top paper and break chocolate into pieces.

INSTANT STRAWBERRY WHIP (*Parve*)

Originally used only on Passover, this Pomerantz treasure graces many a dessert table.

1 cup fresh strawberries (cut up)	1 cup sugar
	1 egg white

Place all ingredients in a mixing bowl. Using an electric mixer, start on slow speed and, when mixed, move to highest speed. Whip is ready when it forms peaks. Strawberry Whip holds up amazingly well. It can be made in advance and refrigerated. Other fresh fruits such as peaches or bananas may be substituted for strawberries. Instant Strawberry Whip may be spooned into pretty serving bowls and garnished with a whole strawberry or spooned into sponge cake or angel food cake. One recipe serves 12 to 20.

MOCHA FLUFF (Dairy)

Delicious served with sponge cake or pound cake.

1 pint whipping cream	1/4 cup sugar
3 T. cocoa	1 T. instant coffee

Beat cream until thick. Gradually mix in cocoa, coffee and sugar.

CHAPTER VIII

ASSORTED MENUS

The most poetic view of marital sex comes from the Zohar, the major work of the Kabbalah movement, which portrays a male as incomplete without a female. The Mishnah, however, takes a very practical view, not poetic but "bookkeeping," you might say.

The marital duty as set forth in the Torah is:
> for men who have no occupation, every day;
> for laborers, twice a week;
> for donkey-drivers [who travel about during the week], once a week
> for camel-drivers [who travel for long periods], once every thirty days;
> for sailors [who may travel for months], once in six months.

-Mishnah, tractate Ketubot, chapter 5, mishnah 5

- Aunt Babette's Menus
- Celebration Menus
- Low-Fat Menus
- Sample Menus from this Book
- Let's Make a Kosher Shower

Note: Menus including items for which recipes are not included in this volume are intended for your enjoyment only!

Better is a dinner of herbs where love is,
Than a stalled ox and hatred therewith.
Better is a dry morsel and quietness therewith,
Than a house full of feasting with strife.
                              Proverbs 15:17; 17:1

AUNT BABETTE'S MENUS
Aunt Babette's Cookbook

BILLS OF FARE

MENU FOR MONDAY
Breakfast

Fruit	Bread
Oat Meal	Butter
Boiled Eggs	Coffee

Lunch

Cold Roast or Poultry	Preserves
Baked or Fried Potatoes	Tea
Pickles	Cake

Dinner

Roast Veal	Prunes
Baked Sweet Potatoes	Cake
Horseradish	Tea
Beets	Coffee

MENU FOR TUESDAY
Breakfast

French Toast	Fruit
Syrup	Coffee

Lunch

Farina Soup	Stewed Tomatoes
Roast Mutton, with Jelly	Pickles
Potatoes	Peach Pie

Supper

Papricash	Canned Plums
Graham Muffins	Tea
Chocolate Soufflé	Coffee

MENU FOR WEDNESDAY
Breakfast

Fruit	Butter
Omelets	Coffee
Bread	

Lunch

Green Kern Soup	Lemon Pie
Breast of Mutton,	Fruit
with Carrots	

Supper

Veal Cutlets	Coffee
Green Peas	Floating Island
Mashed Potatoes	Cup Cake
Tea	

MENU FOR THURSDAY
Breakfast

Fruit	Coffee
Potato Pancakes	Chocolate
Steak	

Lunch

Soup *Schwamchen*	*Kartoffel Kloesse*
Brisket of Beef	Apple Sauce or
Sauer Kraut	Baked Apples

Supper

Mutton Chops   Cake
Baked Sweet Potatoes   Tea or Coffee
Neapolitan Blanc Mange

MENU FOR FRIDAY
Breakfast
Fruit   Oat Meal
Poached Eggs on Toast   Coffee

Lunch
Barley Soup   Canned Corn
Fried Calf's Liver   Beets
Velvet Potato Puffs   Pickles

Supper
Speckled Trout   Prunes
Potatoes   Pistachio Cream
Various Kinds of Coffee   Coffee
  Cake   Apple *Mohn*
Cheese   Chocolate

MENU FOR SATURDAY
Breakfast
Fruits   *Kuchen*
Fried Perch   Coffee

Lunch
Noodle Soup, with   Potatoes
  Chicken   Pickled Pears
Young Duck, with   Cocoanut Pie
  Cauliflower

Supper

Marinirter Herring or Herring Salad	Cake
	Apple Snowballs
Potatoes Cooked in Their Jackets	Coffee

MENU FOR SUNDAY

Breakfast

Sweetbreads	Coffee
Olives	Toast

Lunch

Soup a la Julienne	Asparagus
Roast Turkey	Cold Slaw
Cranberries	Stewed Tomatoes
Beef, with Horseradish Sauce	Plum Pudding
	Roman Sauce
Sweet Potatoes	

Supper

Cold Turkey	Neapolitan Fruit
Neapolitan Salad	Cake
Coffee	

Plain Sunday Dinner

Noodle Soup	Pickled Peaches
Fish, Sweet and Sour	Mustard Pickles
Ducks, Dressed with Bread	Suet Pudding Cooked with Pears
Red Cabbage	Coffee
Sweet Potatoes	

TOP TEN CELEBRATION MENUS

Hey, you never know. It always pays to be prepared!

1.   HAVING A SPECIAL BIRTHDAY --

Grilled portobello mushrooms
Sizzling garlic steak
10-ingredient fried rice
Roasted pecan asparagus
Apple strudel

2.   PLANTING A GARDEN --

Macaroni and cheese
Carrot sticks and black olives
Hot fudge sundaes

3.   BUYING A HOME --

Peanut butter and jelly sandwiches
Celery sticks
Chocolate-chip cookies
Fresh strawberries

4.   ENJOYING GREAT SEX --

Cucumber cups with caviar and champagne
BBQ teriyaki steak with herbed potatoes
String beans with cashew nuts
Chocolate fudge cake with rasperry sauce
Espresso
Mints

Come For Everything ... But *Cholent*

5.   GETTING A RAISE --

An all GREEN menu of:
Green salad
Spinach gnocchi with pesto
Broccoli with scallions
Creamed leeks
Lime jello
Green tea

6.   LEARNING TO SKI --

Hot chocolate fondue
Tortellini with smoked salmon
   and dried tomatoes
Salad of mixed vegetables and raddicchio
Mulled apple cider

7.   TAKING A CRUISE --

Don't ask!!

8.   WINNING AT TENNIS --

Gazpacho
Broiled salmon steaks
Rice with vermicelli
Candied carrots
Apple pie with melted cheese and ice cream

---

9.   WRITING A BOOK --

All Finger Foods:
Fresh fruits
Stuffed mushrooms
Sweetbread tartlets
BBQ chicken wings
Sweet and sour meat balls
Fried *kreplah*
Pickles, olives, hot peppers
Fresh veggies
ALL CHOCOLATE *parve* desserts

10.   WINNING THE LOTTERY --

Artichoke hearts with macademia nut dressing
Thick juicy rib steak smothered in vidalia onions
Couscous with vegetable medley
Oriental eggplant with garlic sauce
Tiramisu (*parve*) and coffee
Sabra liqueur

... and FOR ANY OCCASION --

MAKE RESERVATIONS!

EASY AND HEALTHY LOW-FAT MENUS
(Fish)

These delightful menus by my friend and partner
in Jewish education, Rabbi Shelley Kniaz, are
versatile -- elegant enough for a *Shabbat* meal and
readily informal for casual, mid-week dining.

1.   Salad
      Asparagus, steamed lightly
      Salmon
             Sprinkle on onion and garlic pow-
             der and pepper, broil until still
             moist inside
      Rosemary New Potatoes
             Spray pan with olive oil spray.
             Cover and cook potatoes over low
             heat until done, stirring occasion-
             ally. Sprinkle potatoes with garlic
             and onion powder, pepper and
             rosemary.
      Fresh Fruit
      Frozen Yogurt Pie
             Bake frozen pie crust according to
             printed directions and let cool.
             Soften frozen yogurt and spoon
             into cooled crust. Put into freezer
             until approximately 15 minutes
             before serving. (For *parve* meals,
             use *parve* ice cream.)

2.   Salad
      Steamed Broccoli
      Marinated Tuna Steaks
            Cut thick. Marinate overnight (in
            refrigerator) or simply pour mari-
            nade over steaks and broil:
                  dry red wine
                  tamari sauce
                  onion and garlic powder
                  powdered ginger
                  pepper
            Broil only until still red in center.
      Baked Potatoes
      Non-fat vanilla or lemon yogurt with
      fresh berries

3.   Crudité
      Brook Trout
            Brush inside of trout with olive oil
            and sprinkle with onion and garlic
            powder, rosemary and lemon juice.
            Broil. Serve with wedge of lemon.
      Risotto Pasta
      Miniature zucchini and summer squash,
      steamed
      Raspberry sorbet with sliced bananas

SAMPLE MENUS
From recipes in this volume

1. Cheese Spoon Dumplings with Red
          Pepper Sauce
    Asparagus Leek Soup
    Poached Fish
    Sour Cream Noodle *Kugel*
    Salad or Steamed Broccoli

2. Cucumber Cups with Tabouli
    Halibut Cheeks with Pasta and Sun-Dried
          Tomatoes
    Spinach Soufflé
    Salad or Fresh String Beans

3. Blueberry Soup (*parve*)
    Fall-Apart Chicken
    Carrot Ring
    Rice Casserole

4. Mock Chopped Liver, Israeli Style
    Curried Lamb
    Kale in Browned Garlic
    Potato *Kugel*

LET'S MAKE A KOSHER SHOWER!

Setting up a kosher home is not at all difficult. Rabbi Shelley Kniaz shares a special way to celebrate the occasion.

"In the last ten years, our congregation (Town and Village/Tifereth Israel in New York City) has been blessed with an "epidemic" of members deciding to *kasher* their homes. (I say "epidemic" because it is most definitely "catching.") Our members are wonderful *baalei haḥnasat orḥim* -- continually welcoming guests into their homes. As their fellow congregants experience this, the desire to reciprocate and to do the same for others grows, leading to the decision to have a kosher home. Our rabbi, Larry Sebert, is quick to rush over for a "kosher kitchen consult" as soon as this desire is made known.

These decisions are seen as opportunities to celebrate and show support. And, just as when a couple marries and "sets up house," there are many little and big things the owner of a newly kosher kitchen will need. Thus was the "Kosher Kitchen Shower" created. One or two close friends of the "newly kosher" congregant compile a list of what is needed for the kitchen and set a date for the shower. Thirty or so friends are invited by phone, each one choosing a gift to bring from the list of needed items. The party itself is an exciting and *freilaḥ* event. It's fun, helpful, practical and it's a *mitzvah*! (And don't forget, volunteering to help for a couple hours with cleaning, sorting and *kashering* can be an added gift.) Here are some items that may be

---

useful and appreciated, but it is best to get a list directly from the "source" -- the owner(s) of the kitchen. Many of these items can be purchased in "meat" and "milk" varieties.

can openers
cheese grater
cutting boards
trivets
hot pads
kitchen towels
"milk" and "meat" labels for drawers and
    cabinets
decorative _hallah_ cover
hallah board and knife
plastic storage containers
dishes (check for pattern)
knives
pots and pans
kosher cookbooks (such as _Come For Cholent,_
    Come For Cholent Again and _Come For_
    Everything But Cholent)
ritual washing cup and special towel
utensils: spatula, slotted spoons, mixing spoons,
    etc.
sink racks or basins
dish-drying racks
birkat hamazon booklets (_benchers_)
(Silverware and glasses are likely to be _kashered_,
    but check to see.)
A Guide to Jewish Religious Practice, Isaac Klein
The Jewish Dietary Laws, Dresner and Siegel
(Both books are available by mail from the United Synagogue Book Service, 212-533-7800, x 2003. Or, check your local Jewish bookstore or synagogue giftshop.)"

CHAPTER IX

THE ULTIMATE (honestly!) CHOLENT CHAPTER

Friday night, the beginning of the Sabbath, is regarded as a time of intense spirituality, and, with it, physical -- including sexual -- enjoyment.

> Suppose a man wants to change occupations from a donkey-driver to camel-driver [which keeps him away from home longer, although it pays more]?
>
> The answer: A woman prefers less money with enjoyment to more money with abstinence.
>
> How often should scholars perform their marital duty? Rabbi Judah said in the name of Samuel: Every Friday night.
>
> *-Babylonian Talmud, tractate Ketubot, page 62b*

CHOLENT AS DIGITAL CONVERGENCE

Nothing is simply what it seems anymore. We are entering the era of multi-functionality, many things in one tiny package. In terms of technology, Bill Gates, the brilliant founder of Microsoft, has described this phenomenon in a recent speech as a "digital convergence." He predicts that all information, whether books, catalogues, art or movies, will be put into digital form and made available in portable devices that look like televisions. This consolidation will be a major theme of the 21st Century. I plan to share my information on *cholent* with him as a case in point. *Cholent* is a one-dish meal that is completely filling. Its stories are captivating, yet *cholent* induces sleep. It can be thrown together quickly and efficiently, yet it requires hours of patient, nostril-filling anticipation. In addition, *cholent* has sustained and consolidated our people for thousands of years. As we move into the 21st Century, let us celebrate the multi-functionality of *cholent,* for it truly is many things in one!

CHOLENT AT OXFORD

Professor David Weitzman and his friend Alan Solomon launched the Oxford *Choolant* Society's first dinner on March 6, 1956 after the Society's founding in November 1955.

"So was a tradition started and flourished essentially unchanged for around 30 years, only the cost to members suffering the ravages of time and inflation. The Society's success far surpassed our youthful founding hopes. We never imagined it would survive to challenge three decades of Oxonian intestines. So its current demise is a source of great sorrow to many of us and we can only hope and pray that this will only prove a temporary hiatus before the re-birth of a new era of *Choolant* society vigour. After all, the past was not entirely without turmoil. The anti-bean revolt of the late 50's comes immediately to mind. A group within the Society urged the exclusion of beans from the *Choolant*, while others, true to the faith, deemed beans to be an irremovable ingredient of the dish. A conflict to tax the wisdom even of Solomon! The ingenuity of *Choolanteers*, however, knows no bounds, and by keeping the beans to the outer regions of the stewpot, and the central region bean-free, honour was satisfied and peace restored. The wind has been taken out of the bean revolt!

Old *Choolanteers* are spread across the globe and have taken their peculiar treasure to the ends of the earth. Flaunting their society ties -- a *Choolant* pot surmounted by a crossed knife and fork -- they are proud to proclaim their alimentary allegiance!"

AVIS WEITZMAN'S *CHOLENT*

As served to her husband David and their sons.

"Like all the best food, *choolant* is all things to all people. Some make it watery, others like a thick soup. Some use it as a vegetable side dish along with a meat or chicken entrée, but the best *Choolant* is served as a main course and a very delicious one! You can make it from all sorts of good things -- you can even make a vegetarian *choolant* that is a very satisfactory main dish. Sephardim put in whole eggs and chickpeas, but *choolant* is essentially a European dish.

As with other peasant foods, quantities are never exact. Did you ever ask your grandmother how to make a cake? She'd say: "Use eggs, flour and sugar," and when you asked "How much?," she'd say "You'll see how much goes in!" It's the same with *choolant*. Here is a real *Ashkenazi* recipe.

1 potato per person

1 handful of butter beans }   there is no
1 handful of haricot beans }   need to soak
1 handful of pearl barley }   these

a large piece of chuck roast	large pinch of paprika
large pinch of cinnamon	1 whole onion, peeled
large pinch of ginger	1 T. honey
	pepper and generous quantity of salt

→

Put meat in bottom of large casserole with tight-fitting lid, cover with beans and onion. Add spices, salt, pepper and honey. Cover completely with water (be generous, as the beans and barley will absorb a lot and much will evaporate during the cooking). Cover tightly. Put into a medium-temperature oven (350°) well before *Shabbat* starts. Just before *Shabbat* comes in, turn heat way down (200°) and leave on overnight. When you wake up on *Shabbat* morning, the delicious smell will fill the whole house. By lunch-time it will be thick, brown and wonderful.

Betayavon -- a hearty appetite."

THE CAMBRIDGE *CHOLENT* SOCIETY

Steve Kraus, principal of Adath Jeshurun, Elkins Park, PA, phoned to alert me to *Cholent* on the Web! I told my son-in-law, Stephen Boro, in San Diego, and he has been corresponding with Michael Jaeger, the president of the Cambridge *Cholent* Society.

"The Society was founded in 1993. At the time, I held the position of Canteen Manager (meaning I was in charge of food in the Jewish Society) and found it a bit of a waste to throw away the remains of the *cholent* after *Shabbat* lunch. Therefore, I returned it to the covered flame and we ate it for *seudah shlishit*. I had heard of the Oxford *Cholent* Society. Hence, this eating of *cholent* was transformed into a meeting of the Cambridge University *Cholent* Society.

We eat *cholent* late on a *Shabbat* afternoon, but we have a very strong *cholent* philosophy. We argue violently with the practice of the Oxford *Cholent* Society, which dines on *cholent* once a term in the middle of the week. We object on several points:

Firstly, *cholent* should be a food for the people and not for a select group alone.

Secondly, eating *cholent* once a term cannot be deemed an appreciation of *cholent*.

And thirdly, and most definitely the most offending point, *cholent* cannot be eaten in the middle of the week! Real *cholent* only exists on *Shabbat*, and tastes, smells, looks, feels and even sounds different during the week. We feel very strongly about our *cholent*!

We have had media coverage, too. We appeared in the University newspaper at the beginning of the year and there was also an article mentioning us in the *Jewish Chronicle* (the national Jewish paper) a couple of weeks ago. At the beginning of this year, we had a stall at the University Society's Fair at which we gave out over 500 bowls of *cholent*.

Enjoy the *cholent* recipe from Jerusalem on the next page."

Michael Jaeger,
INTERNET:93mdj@eng.cam.ac.uk

Thanks to Michael Jaeger, this recipe comes straight off the web, courtesy of the Information Division of the Israel Foreign Ministry, Jerusalem.

"*Cholent*, a heavy stew, became the answer to the age-old problem of how to have nourishing hot food on the Sabbath without violating injunctions in Jewish traditional law. Since it is permitted to prepare food in advance and keep it warm in an oven lit before the Sabbath began, *cholent*, which is not impaired by long, slow cooking (indeed the process improves the flavor), was adopted as the principal *Shabbat* food in Eastern Europe.

In Israel, *cholent* has become exceedingly popular with every segment of the population. There are even restaurants where one sees lines of customers standing with pot-in-hand waiting for their turn to get "take-home" *cholent*.

Cholent is served only on weekends. Anyone who partakes of this dish will understand why. It is a thick, heavy, and filling food which induces sleep.

2 cups dried lima beans	2 T flour
3 lbs. brisket	8 small potatoes (peeled)
3 onions, diced	1 cup pearled barley
2 t. paprika	8 eggs (uncooked)
1/4 t. pepper	2 t. salt
1/4 t. ginger	2 T. fat or margarine

Soak the beans overnight in water. Drain. Use a heavy saucepan or Dutch oven and brown meat and onions in the fat (or margarine). Sprinkle with salt, pepper and ginger. Add beans, barley, small potatoes (peeled) and sprinkle with flour and paprika. Place uncooked eggs in shells on top. Add enough boiling water to cover one inch above the mixture. Cover tightly. *Cholent* may be baked for 24 hours at 250° or for quicker cooking, bake at 350° for 4-5 hours. Serves 8-10."

FRUIT COMPOTE CHOLENT*

Purists will not condone calling this *cholent*, but *by me* it's close enough!

To a crock pot, add:
1 17-oz. can peach halves, drained
1 17-oz. can sliced pears, drained
1 17-oz.can pineapple chunks, drained

1 17-oz.can apricot halves, drained
2 21-oz. cans cherry pie filling
2 sticks cinnamon
a splash or two of brandy

Cook on low for 4-5 hours. Remove cinnamon sticks prior to serving.

Serve as a main dish, side dish, or as a hot dessert.

*If prepared for *Shabbat*, due to increased time, add 1 1/2 cans drained fruit juice.

CHOLENT ABUSE IS THE NEWEST JEWISH HORROR
by Allan Gould

Cholent. If you're not from a traditional Jewish background, you may not be aware of this remarkable ethnic treat. Potatoes, beans, onions, and -- if your family belonged to the Polish Jewish aristocracy -- hunks of meat, all placed on a hot stove or in a heated oven and cooked for long hours from Friday on, so religious Jews would have something warm to eat on the Sabbath, without having to light a fire.

But headlines around the world have shown rising fear over a tragic new Jewish horror, *Cholent* Abuse.

Cholent Abuse could be affecting your children, but before you panic, take a deep breath, cut out and paste on your fridge these Telltale Signs, just below the wonderful drawings of your gifted youngsters, *keineinhora*.

Telltale Signs of *Cholent* Abuse
-Chronic stomach upset and bulging stomach.
-A sudden change of friends, from vegetarians to meat-eaters.
-Spotting your child stealing potatoes, beans, and often (but not always) massive hunks of cheap brisket, and discovering that your largest meat pots are missing.
-The inability of your child to eat *milhik* meals.
-Wild mood swings, from complaining of

overeating, to complaining of overeating.

-Frequent belching, burping and mumbling "mehayah."

-Loss of interest in discussing anything with family except the cost of potatoes and beans; the high price of kosher meat; the difficulty in finding quality Spanish onions at the market; etc.

-Always having his/her lunch made for school, but refusing to show it to you when you ask.

-Hanging around his/her *bubbie's* house, begging endlessly for something to eat -- especially on Sabbath afternoons.

Look. You're not a failure as a parent. You're not helpless. And you are certainly not alone.

If you think you're a failure, consider these facts: There are many kids with neglectful Jewish parents who never even touch *cholent*. And there are also children with seemingly model Jewish parents who do abuse *cholent*.

The first thing to accept is, while *cholent* is indeed dangerous and can be fatal, it is simply one more problem that Jewish children have to handle, from endless *bar mitzvah* parties in their early teens, to tremendous pressure on 15-year-old girls to "get married, already."

The Aware Jewish Parent Is The Good Jewish Parent

There are no symptoms which are absolutely reliable in spotting *cholent* abuse. But there are clues, as you have seen in our telltale signs above.

Don't jump to conclusions, even if that's the only exercise you get around your house. Many of these warning signs for *cholent* abuse are the same as those for *greben* grabbing, *kneidle* and *kugel* craving, and *latke* loving. It's all part of the ups and downs of being a Jewish teenager.

Start Within Your Family
Everything must start with a frank discussion. It's crucial that you speak frankly with your child about the possibility of *cholent* abuse. And it's particularly important to talk about your values, and why you are dead set against the overeating of *cholent* -- even after *shul* on *Shabbat*.

If your youngster seems evasive, or the explanations are unconvincing, you may wish to consult a good Jewish doctor, preferably one who is not hooked on *cholent*.

You might also wish to have your child visit a *cholent* professional, such as *bubbie*, to see if she can help.

Whatever You Do, Never Give Up Hope!
Don't you forget: That child who now seems to be grotesquely indulging in *cholent* is the same boy or girl who, only a few years ago, gave you such joy at their *bar* or *bat mitzvah*. Someday, he or she could find the cure for the Heartbreak of Psoriasis, or win the Nobel Prize for Physics. But the kid needs your help now, more than ever before.

For more information on how to talk with your Jewish child about *cholent* abuse, you can obtain a free copy of "A Jewish Parent's Guide to Stopping *Cholent* Overuse" by calling 1-800-CHOLENT.

(Allan Gould is the author of 18 books, including the scholarly What Did They Think Of The Jews? *and the very funny anthology,* The Great Big Book of Canadian Humour. *He tries to avoid* cholent *at all times, except on* Shabbat *afternoons; otherwise, he'd sleep 20 hours a day. Which is another telltale sign, now that he thinks about it.)*

C IS FOR *CHOLENT*

A=   is for <u>a</u> little, of this and of that,
B=   is for beans, they won't make you fat.

C=   is for *cholent*, on *Shabbat* it's a stew,
D=   don't forget potatoes, whatever you do.

E=   eat your *cholent* with a fork or a spoon,
F=   fill your bowl and then hum a tune.

G=   grate in an onion, it might make you cry,
H=   hold your nose and don't ask me why.

I=   in a pan, some garlic you'll fry,
J=   just for aroma, a really good buy.

K=   *kishke* is good to throw into the pot,
L=   layer it with veggies and let it get hot.

M=   mix some ketchup with sugar and spice,
N=   never forget to add a cup of rice.

O=   open some olives, the pitted ones are best,
P=   put them in the crockpot with all the rest.

Q=   quick as can be, your *cholent's* on its way,
R=   ready for *Shabbat* and each holiday.

S=   slowly it'll cook, all day and all night,
T=   the trick is knowing it's *always* just right.

U=   utmost importance -- add cold water too,
V=   veggies and/or meat, whatever you do.

W=   whatever you do, wherever you go,
X=   x marks the spot your tummy will know!

Cholent is delicious from A to Z. Won't you come
have some with me?

A RESPONSE FROM A *CHOLENT* FAN
Judy Resnick, Far Rockaway, NY

"Reading through two thousand years of rabbinical discourses on the Sabbath laws regarding *"bishul"* (warming food) and *"hatmanah"* (insulating food) gives one an insightful look into what was eaten by Jews of different lands and times. For instance, Rabbi Shimon Eider relates in his modern compilation of *"Hilchos Shabbos"* that three kinds of stoves were known to the Sages of the Talmud. The *kirah* stove was long and rectangular, the *kupach* stove was cube-shaped, and the *tanur* stove was pyramidal. Of these, the *kirah* stove was closest in design and function to the stoves used today. The discussions in Tractate Sabbath (and later, in the Code of Jewish Law) form the basis for many holiday and Sabbath meal customs (including *blech* and *cholent*).

As you have said in your cookbook(s), *"cholent"* is really any collection of different tastes and textures that can survive many hours of cooking over low heat. The excellent young-adult novel by June Leavitt, *The Flight to Seven Swan Bay* (Feldheim Publishers), tells how fifteen observant Jews stranded in the wilderness of the Pacific Northwest manage to survive and even make *"cholent"* for *Shabbos*. The intrepid travelers outwit a bear, trap a deer and prepare venison-and-Jerusalem-artichoke *cholent*!

Another Feldheim author, Racoma Shain, describes in the partly autobiographical *All for the Boss* her life in the small Yeshiva town of Mir, Poland, during

---

the 1930s. Cooking over the tiny "primus stove" (spirit lamp) or in the large *"kachal* stove" (fireplace) was an impossible task, but their *Shabbos cholent* was always perfect. Young *balabusta* Mrs. Shain would bring her pot of *"brust* meat" (flanken) and *"perel groipen"* (barley) to the town baker before *Shabbos,* who would bank his huge oven with coals and let all the Mir housewives' *cholent* pots simmer there. Sadly, this world came to an end when the Nazis invaded Mir in 1941.

The bestseller by Frances Moore Lappé, *Diet For a Small Planet,* and its companion, *Recipes For a Small Planet,* introduced the idea of "complementary proteins." According to Mrs. Lappé, the proteins in meat and legumes and vegetables complement each other, so that serving the admixtures like casseroles or stews enhances and extends the protein value of the meat. Therefore, small amounts of meat should be combined with lots of different legumes and vegetables in order to stretch the maximum use of protein from the minimum use of Earth's resources. So, *cholent* is good for you and for the planet! (But you knew that already.) Mrs. Lappé would probably love *cholents* that call for high-protein turkey and soybeans added to various grains or roots such as kasha and burdock.

Awfully amusing to note how one culture's "native cooking" (i.e., the stuff thrown together by poor housewives from what was cheap and available) turns into another culture's "trendy cuisine." It happened with African-American soul food, bouillabaisse, jambalaya and burritos. Now it's happening with the lowly *cholent.* A well-known yuppie guidebook raved about a dish called cassoulet, which turned out to be nothing more than a glorified and overpriced *cholent* made from duck and white beans.

The popular Jewish satire-and-kiddie-songs group, Country Yossi and the Shteeble-Hoppers (I did not make that up!), has a number of records and cassettes which have sold well in the *"Yiddishe olam."* One of their songs is, naturally, the *Cholent* Song! I can only remember the line, *"Cholent*-powered rockets will take men to the moon," and the refrain, *"ch-ch-ch-cholent."*

As you've perceptively observed in your cookbooks, *cholent* is about sharing and caring and warmth and love. *Cholent* can be made for five or five hundred -- but it can't be made for one. *B'tayavon* and best wishes!"

If, after eating, you do not walk four cubits before bed, your food will stay undigested.

Rashi

THE ESSENCE OF *CHOLENT*

Just when I thought there were no new *cholent* surprises, I came across a copy of a children's book, *Cholent*, by Peter Syle, Pitspopany Press, 1994. In it, *cholent* is defined as a native of the planet Yapzug. *Cholent* emits a toxic shmertz gas as a by-product of its breathing!" According to the author, this definition comes from the Earth Prime Edition of the Intergalactic Dictionary! The contents lists nine chapters, including The Last *Cholent*, Well Done!, Blue Bean Bubble-bursts, Acid and Antacid, etc. In this sci-fi story, the *cholent*, nearly conscious, experiences an earthquake on Yapzug, crashes into titanium rods and hides under a control panel. I don't want to give away the entire plot, but suffice it to say, others may perish but the *cholent* survives. And you thought I had a wild imagination!

CHAPTER X

SUSHI

Food should be appetizing as well as nourishing.
Talmud

STEPHEN'S SUSHI SMORGASBORD

Sushi has become a "passion" for most of our family. Stephen, our son-in-law, has it down to a science.

Preparation time: 1 hour
Serves: 2 gluttons for dinner

4 humans for dinner, with miso soup, green tea, and ice cream
8-12 for appetizers

Ingredients:

3 cups short-grain Japanese "sticky" rice
3 cups water
8 T. rice vinegar
1 package Nori (seaweed wrappers)
sweet pickled ginger (garnish)
sesame seeds
4 roma tomatoes
2 ripe avocados

1 cucumber, peeled
1 package artificial crab (no natural flavorings)
1 sweet red onion
1/4 lb. lox
1/4 cup mayonnaise
3 T. wasabi (green horseradish)
soy sauce

Equipment:

small stockpot or rice cooker
sharp knife
cutting board

9" x 13" casserole dish
paper plate
clean moist dish towel

The rice:
Once you have gathered all your ingredients, start

making the rice. The rice is the most daunting element of the entire project, causing the most seasoned cooks to throw up their hands in frustration and go looking for "Uncle Ben." I say, "Fear not!" There are just a few simple things to remember when preparing the perfect batch of sushi rice:

1) The rice is supposed to be sticky.
2) The rice needs to relax in the water before it's boiled.
3) Never, ever, ever, lift up the lid while the rice is cooking.

Keeping in the tradition of the master sushi chefs, I use an electric (gasp!) rice cooker. This device has been a boon to me in that it makes perfect rice every time. All you do is add equal amounts of rice and water, let them soak for 30 minutes, and then turn on the machine. Fifteen minutes later you have rice ready to be molded into your favorite sushi.

Without a rice cooker:
Making the perfect sushi rice without a rice cooker is not an insurmountable problem. You will need a fairly large saucepan or small stockpot. Follow the directions on the bag, and you will have perfect rice. Remembering the three rules above, the directions should say:

1) Soak the rice for 30 minutes.
2) Cover the pot.
3) Bring to a boil then lower the heat to simmer.
4) Simmer for 20 minutes.
5) Remove from heat immediately.

While the rice is cooking, prepare your ingredients. Chop the cucumber and imitation crab into a

---

nice julienne, not too thin. The tomatoes, avocado, and red onion can be cut a little thicker, but the idea is for them to end up in strips as well. One of the reasons I like to use roma tomatoes in this recipe is their oblong shape, making them well suited for cutting lengthwise. However, if roma tomatoes are unavailable, feel free to use whatever type you have. The lox should be cut into strips as well.

By now, your rice should be ready. Open the lid, but be very careful of escaping steam. Transfer the rice to the casserole dish, spreading it out evenly. There may be some golden, crunchy rice in the bottom of the pot. This is your treat for working so hard in the kitchen. Munch on it while preparing the rest of the dish, but don't put it in the casserole dish.

What we do now is known as "fanning" the rice. (If you have a significant other, now is the time to enlist his/her help.) With one hand holding a paper plate, begin to fan the rice in the casserole. With your other hand, turn the rice gently with a large spoon, fanning as you go. Pause for a moment to introduce the rice vinegar evenly about the dish. Continue fanning and turning, trying to assure an even distribution of the vinegar. Touch the rice. If you burn your hand, continue fanning. When the rice is comfortable to the touch, we begin to make the sushi!

Place a sheet of Nori on your work surface. Spoon some rice onto the sheet of Nori. How much rice you spoon on is a matter of personal preference.

The more rice you add, the fatter your sushi roll will be. Since we are adding many vegetables, I like a little bit less rice in my roll. Spread the rice out to a thickness of 1/4 inch. You may go over the edges on three sides, but the fourth side (one of the long sides) must leave about 1 inch of Nori showing:

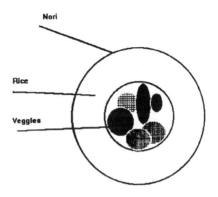

Once rolled, the sushi log must be sliced into 8 pieces with a very sharp dampened knife. If your log is rolled tightly enough, you shouldn't have to worry about it losing its shape when sliced. I like to cut the log in half, put the pieces together and halve them again, and then cut each of the pieces in half. Keep repeating until all the rice is gone. Presentation is as important as the food in Japanese cooking. Arrange the pieces nicely on a platter, decorate with some wasabi and sweet pickled ginger.

Sushi pieces may be eaten with your fingers or with chopsticks. Remember, though, that these are meant to be bite-sized pieces, and the whole piece should be plopped into your mouth. In the privacy of your own home, who's to know?

The sushi pieces may be dipped in soy sauce. Some people add wasabi and sweet pickled ginger to the soy sauce to flavor it. Some dab the wasabi right on the sushi. Others place a slice of sweet pickled ginger right on top of the piece of sushi. Still others eat the pickled ginger by itself, as a palate cleanser, between various types of sushi.

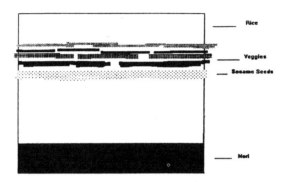

Sprinkle some sesame seeds in a row over the rice, approximately 1/3 of the way down the square. Dab some mayonnaise over it. If you like a bit of a kick for your taste buds, dab some wasabi over it, too. Lay your julienned ingredients over the rice. When all your ingredients have been laid out, it's time to roll it up.

Rolling sushi takes practice. Your first few rolls may end up being just spirals. Don't let this stop you! It will still taste the same. With a finger, dampen the exposed edge of the Nori. This will help it stick when it's all rolled up. With both hands, hold the top edge of the Nori and start rolling toward the exposed edge. With free fingers, hold the veggie row together as you roll. Roll tightly. Ideally, the veggies should be together in the center, surrounded by a ring of rice.

INDEX

This index provides easy access to recipes in this cookbook:

Cucumber
  Cups, 133
  Salad, 133
  Soup, 11

D
Drinks
  Mock Orange Julius,
    139
  Punch
    Champagne,
      122
    Mulled Cider,
      121
    Mulled Wine,
      121
  Russian Tea, 139
  Sangria Supreme,
    122
Dumplings
  Cheese Spoon, 82-83
  Turkey, 60

E
Eggplant Caviar, 87

F,G
Fettucini, Broccoli, 78
Fish
  Chowder, 17
  Citrus, 39
  Cod
    Burgers, 39
    Garlicky Baked,
      31
    With Almonds,
      38
  Gefilte Fish, 34-5
  Halibut Cheeks, 30
  Poached, 29
  Salmon (See
    Salmon)
  Seared Snapper, 36
  Tuna, Babette's, 33
  Tuna, Fresh, 32
  Tuna Salad, 33
Frozen Cheese Salad,
  73
Fruit
  Cholent, 166
  Soup, 13

H,I,J
Halibut (See Fish)
Hamburger Yummy,
  59
Haroset
  Bill Dantzic's, 118-9
  Instant *Haroset*, 119
Herring
  Soup, 17
  With *Schnapps*, 37
Horseradish, Beet, 134

K
Kale with Browned
  Garlic, 89
Kosher Shower, 155-6

Omelette, Overnight,
75
Orange Roughy (See
Fish)

P,Q
Parsnips, Orange, 91
Peanut Soup, 12
Peppers, Pickled, 135
Pomerantzen (Candied
Fruit Peel), 127
Preserves, Black
Radish, 117
Punch
Champagne, 122
Cider, 121
Wine, 121

R
Radish, Black Radish
Preserves, 117
Raspberry Sauce, 137
Rice
Casserole, 83
Spanish, 134
Ribs
Chinese-Style, 57
Lamb Barbecue, 57
Rutabagas, 90

S
Salad
Fiesta, 74
Chicken, 48
Salmon

Marinated, 26
Pickled, 26
Poached, 28
Seattle, 23
Sweet and Sour, 27
Sauce
Raspberry, 137
Salsa Verde, 136
Sandwich -- Grilled
Cheese and
Artichoke, 132
Sangria, 122
Soufflé
Spinach, 77
Squash, 111
Zucchini, 110
Soups
Almond Bisque, 16
Asparagus-Leek, 9
Avocado, 10
Blueberry, 6
Buttermilk *Borscht*,
12
Cabbage *Borscht*, 10
Carrot, 8
Chicken, 3-4
Creamed Carrot, 8
Cucumber, 11
Fish Chowder, 17
Fruit, 13
Herring, 17
Minestrone, 15
Mushroom, 16
Peanut, 12
Purim Soup, 14

Come For Everything ... But *Cholent*